Thyssen-Bornemisza Foundation

Thyssen-Bornemisza Foundation Villa Favorita

Guidebook

edited by Maria de Peverelli

Thyssen-Bornemisza Foundation

Skira

Contents

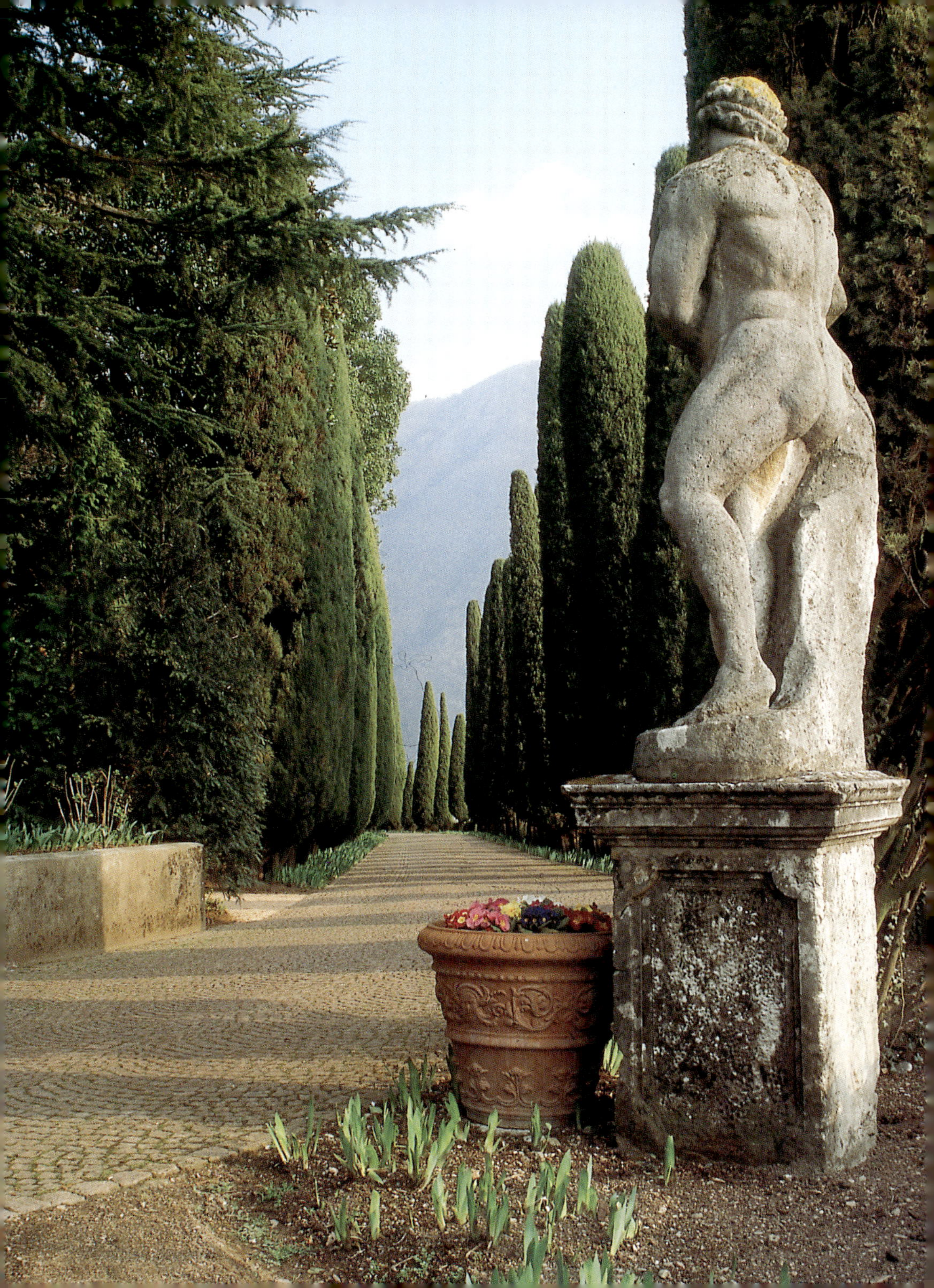

Villa Favorita

A place, two men and a passion. These met on the shore of Lake Lugano and gave birth to the gallery of Villa Favorita. Set in a splendid garden, the gallery is a living witness to the undying love for art of two generations of collectors. The pages of this guide, if only briefly, tell their story.

Entering Villa Favorita at the foot of Mount Bré is like entering a separate, enchanted world with a rarefied atmosphere. Here the contemplation of nature's beauty finds its ideal complement in the works of art that embellish the house and gallery.

The history of Villa Favorita begins in 1687, when Carlo Corrado Beroldingen from the Uri Canton, chancellor to the captain governing the town of Lugano, decided to build a house on this site (the architect's name is unknown). The Beroldingen emblem of two lions on globes may still be admired on the gate in front of the villa, just a few yards from the lake, as well as on the gate at the beginning of the avenue of cypresses. In 1732, the villa changed hands, when Giovanni Rodolfo Riva of Lugano purchased it together with its garden[1]. The Riva coat of arms, a fish and an arm with a sword, can be seen on the wrought-iron railing of the balcony on the villa's facade, the ceiling of one of the ground floor rooms and a fireplace on the first floor.

As Paolo Cottini suggested in his brief guide of the garden of Villa Favorita (1996), the villa may have been named Favorita in imitation of the Gonzaga villa of the same name at Porto Mantovano. The villa remained in the Riva family until 1919 when it was bought by Prince Frederic Leopold of Prussia. The most lasting traces of his ownership are the splendid avenue of cypresses, the two wings that were added laterally to the building's main corpus as well as the transformation of the small pavilion of the Glorietta and the building below into a terraced dwelling joined to the main building by a gallery with busts of various princes[2]. It was his son who sold it in 1932 to Baron Heinrich Thyssen-Bornemisza, who was looking for a "home" for his collection of Old Master paintings. After he had restored the existing buildings and enlarged the garden, he commissioned a gallery, connected both to the villa and to the Glorietta, for his collection.

Today, a long avenue of cypresses (for the most part those planted by Prince Frederic Leopold of Prussia) runs along the lake and leads both to the gallery and the villa, which is set in its terraced garden and seems almost as if it were suspended between the water and the sky. The vast panorama of the lake, the true protagonist of the scene, is unbroken. We only have glimpses of it between the cypresses until it opens in front of us after the first three hundred yards. We can see Mount San Salvatore in all its majesty and Campione, Melide and Lugano forming a distant frame. Springtime, when the garden is a triumph of luxurious rhododendrons, azaleas, camellias, magnolias and wisteria, is the best time to visit Villa Favorita. With its numerous exotic specimens arranged on terraces that descend to the lake—its statues with their allusions to pastoral divinities scattered about to amaze and amuse the visitor in keeping with a long garden tradition—the garden acts like a host who welcomes the visitor and accompanies him on his walk to the gallery. The first among the most interesting plants along the walk to the gallery is a Japanese cypress. This can be seen on the right, just after the caretaker's house together with other evergreens. Soon after this there is a majestic chestnut,

[2] Between 1929 and 1932, Prince Frederic Leopold bought some land at Montalbano. Here he had the architects Clement and Könitz build a villa facing south. This was only inhabited by his son for a short period and is currently a hotel.

Villa Favorita

which is probably the source of the hill's name (chestnut in Italian is *castagno*, hence Castagnola). On the same side, just after the curve in the path that is indicated with a Hercules statue, one may note (in order) a tri-coloured beech, two ginkgoes, a camphor tree and a magnificent tulip tree which is over thirty metres high. Just before the garages (two red buildings), at the end of the cypress avenue, are a locust and an *Osmanto*. At this point, the view of the lake opens before us.

Continuing along, the visitor comes across two small buildings. The first is entirely covered by a false jasmine; an enormous cypress that is a masterpiece of topiary art seems as if it were growing up the building's facade. On the first-floor garden terrace of this building there is a wisteria arbour with terracotta vases set on its pilasters. These vases are repeated as decorative elements on other terraces and balustrades around the property. Beyond the wisteria arbour there is a second building, called the Baby Home. The most interesting element of its decoration is the balustrade of the terrace which is embellished with putti carrying cornucopias and bunches of grapes. On the east wall of the building, over a stone bench, there is a small marble relief of the Madonna and Child with two saints. Another relief depicting Saint Christopher decorates one of the two garages. A third, in glazed terracotta, reminiscent of the works of the Della Robbia family, is visible a few yards beyond on one of the banks supporting the terraces of the garden. The statue of a hunter and a bust of Vespasian, both on pedestals, may also be seen immersed in the greenery nearby.

At the lake level, the garden broadens and we arrive at the old lemon arbour whose supports are decorated by climbing roses. Here we see some stone benches and a large basin decorated with a female bust in marble. In front of the lemon arbour, which was already mentioned in documents dating from 1845, in addition to a group of female statues, there are a Douglas fir, a white magnolia, a dwarf palm, and an imposing horse chestnut. Behind it, higher up, one can see the wall of the gallery.

Proceeding, we find the new lemon arbour, now used as a greenhouse. On the lawn in front, two of the villa's notable guests left mementoes of their visits. In 1985, Princess Margaret of England planted a magnolia that bears her name. For his part, the Dalai Lama left a *Michelia*, a specimen from the Sino-Tibetan magnolia family. Two metal plaques at the feet of the trees commemorate their visits.

This point delimits the public from the private part of the villa's property. To the right on the lake side there is a little well, and on the

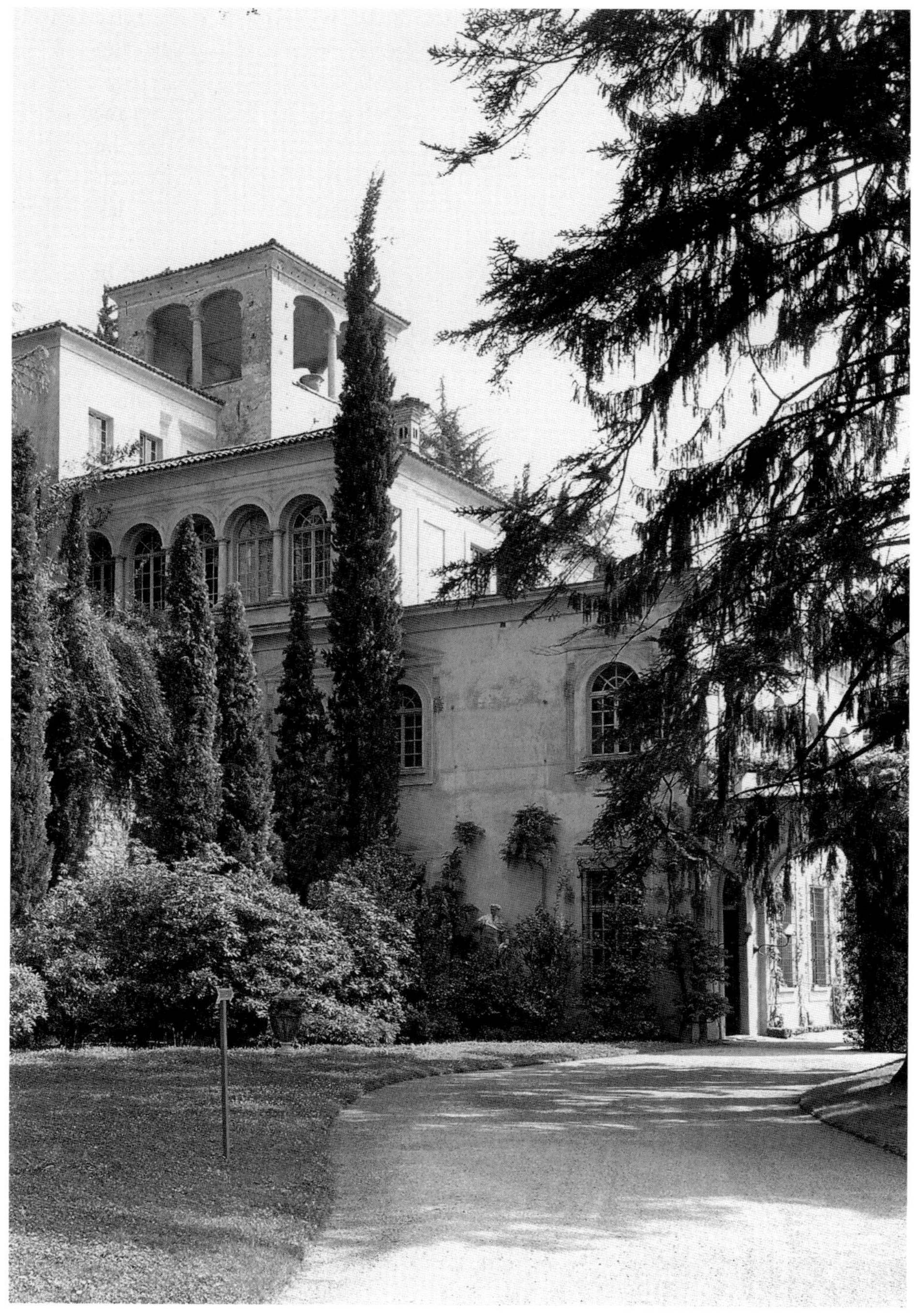

Villa Favorita

left, the Glorietta, a small tower that was erected at the same time as the villa at the end of the seventeenth century. From its terrace the visitor may still enjoy a splendid view of the lake. Restored in the 1960s, the building almost seems to fade into the garden vegetation that climbs its walls and portico.

The area between the Glorietta and the villa is not accessible to visitors (except by reservation, and with an obligatory guided tour), but whoever turns his gaze in this direction will see the three Palladian porticoes supported by the twin columns that characterise the Thyssen-Bornemisza residence. One cannot help but remain enchanted by the natural backdrop created by the imposing Himalayan cypress, the magnolia grandiflora and most of all the two enormous rhododendrons. At the foot of the cedar, the sharp eye can pick out a bronze sculpture by Marino Marini (*Miracle*, 1954) and a bit beyond, to the left next to the stairway that leads to the corridor connecting the gallery to the villa, another work in bronze by Nag Arnoldi of 1980 entitled *The Grand Duke (Owl)*.

From the Glorietta one can reach the gallery that contains a part of the works collected by Baron Hans Heinrich Thyssen-Bornemisza, current owner of the Villa Favorita.

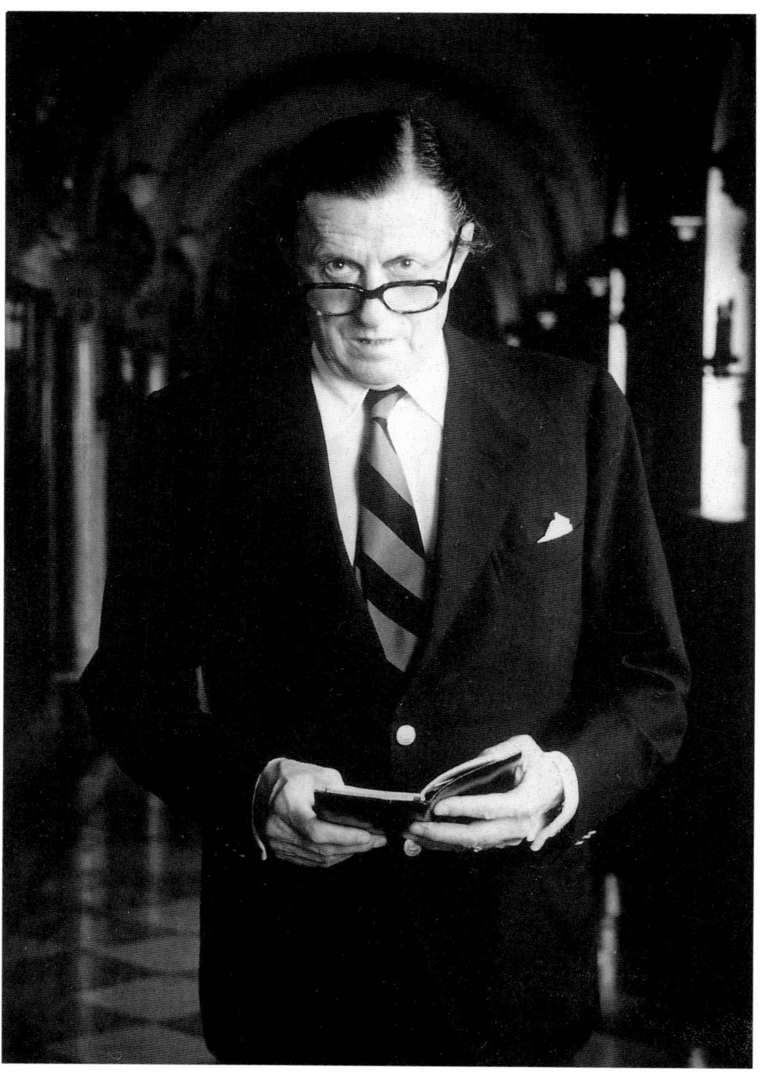

History of the Thyssen-Bornemisza Collection

The Thyssen family came from near Aachen, Germany, and its origins can be traced back to the eighteenth century. The founder of the family's fortune, derived from iron and steel, was August Thyssen (1842-1926). His interest in ancient art was limited to the decoration of his country house, Schloß Landsberg, with copies of the Old Masters. This limit, however, did not prevent him from appreciating the great French sculptor Auguste Rodin. In 1905 he commissioned a series of works in marble by the sculptor that still belong to his descendants. These are the first witnesses to the passion for collecting that grew in the collection of August's son Heinrich and continues with Hans Heinrich, the current Baron Thyssen-Bornemisza.

August Thyssen had seven children, three boys and four girls. The eldest, Fritz, became a well-known industrialist. The second, August, could best be described as a *bon viveur*. The third, Heinrich, who received his degree in philosophy from London University, had little interest in living in his elder brother's shadow and left Germany to live in Hungary. Here he married the daughter of Baron Gabor Bornemisza, an aristocrat who held an important position at the Hungarian court. Heinrich, who became a Hungarian citizen, was adopted by his father in law and obtained the title of Baron. At Schloß Rohoncz, Heinrich led the life of a country gentleman. However with the rise to power of Béla Kun in 1919, he was forced to flee to Holland. The youngest of his four children, the current Baron Hans Heinrich, was born there in 1921.

Hans Heinrich Thyssen-Bornemisza (photo Evelyn Hofer)

Heinrich Thyssen-Bornemisza (1875-1947) should be considered the true founder of the collection. His enormous fortune, his close friendships with men the calibre of Wilhelm von Bode and Max J.

Baron Heinrich Thyssen-Bornemisza in the gallery, circa 1940

Friedländer, and the advice of the noted German antique dealer Rudolf Heinemann, permitted him—by the end of the 1920s—to assemble a large number of masterpieces dating from the fourteenth to the eighteenth centuries. He favoured the German Renaissance and portraiture, and acquired works in this genre by Dürer, Ghirlandaio, Antonello da Messina, Lucas Cranach the Elder, and Carpaccio, among the others. His collection was shown to the public for the first time in 1930 at the Neue Pinakothek in Munich under the name "The Schloß Rohoncz Collection". Praise for the collection, from both the public and critics, was enormous. This success encouraged Heinrich Thyssen-Bornemisza to pursue his activity as a collector and to broaden his interests. In fact, his major acquisitions of goldsmith work, sculpture, furniture and rugs date from this period. The necessity of finding an adequate and secure setting for his collection lead him to purchase Villa Favorita on the shore of Lake Lugano in 1932 and to commission the Swiss architect Hans Geiser to build a gallery (the one that we may visit today.) The gallery was opened to the public in 1936, but the outbreak of war in 1939 forced it to close soon after. Likewise, Heinrich Thyssen-Bornemisza ceased collecting at that time. After dedicating the collection to his father August, he left more than half of it to his younger son, Hans Heinrich. After his father's death, the latter bought most of the works that his brothers and sisters had inherited from their father. In 1948 he reopened the gallery to the public. From then on, he has not only continued to fill in the collection of Old Masters, but he has also extended the collection's range into the nineteenth and twentieth centuries, periods that his father held in low esteem. Nineteenth-century American painting,

History of the Thyssen-Bornemisza Collection

German Expressionism, French and American Impressionism, European avant-garde artists as well as a recent portrait by Lucian Freud have all contributed to the collection's enrichment. By the end of the 1980s, this contained over fifteen hundred paintings and had tripled in size since it was first shown to the public in 1930.

The desire to preserve the fruits of their collecting activities for the future and to keep their collections intact is common to many collectors. Since the gallery at Villa Favorita is only big enough to display three-hundred and fifty works of painting and sculpture at one time, Baron Thyssen-Bornemisza has tried since the mid-1980s to find a space that would permit the showing of, if not all, at least the most important works in his collection; he believes that such works constitute a common cultural and artistic patrimony that should be accessible to as many people as possible. When the King and Queen of Spain put a newly refurbished palace across from the Prado at his disposal to house over seven hundred of his paintings, he was happy to accept this offer as it resolved his problem of the limited space at Villa Favorita. The inauguration of the Thyssen-Bornemisza museum in Madrid took place in 1992. Another core of around sixty paintings hangs in the Pedralbes monastery near Barcelona.

With the departure for Spain of all of the Old Master paintings that once hung there, the gallery of Villa Favorita has had to change its appearance. Today, the rooms in the Glorietta display a series of sculptures along with a few pieces of furniture and Old Master paintings that testify to the collection's origins. The rooms of the actual gallery, however, display around one-hundred and fifty European and American paintings and watercolours from the nineteenth and twentieth centuries. These represent a panoramic view of the fields that interest the gallery's current owner.

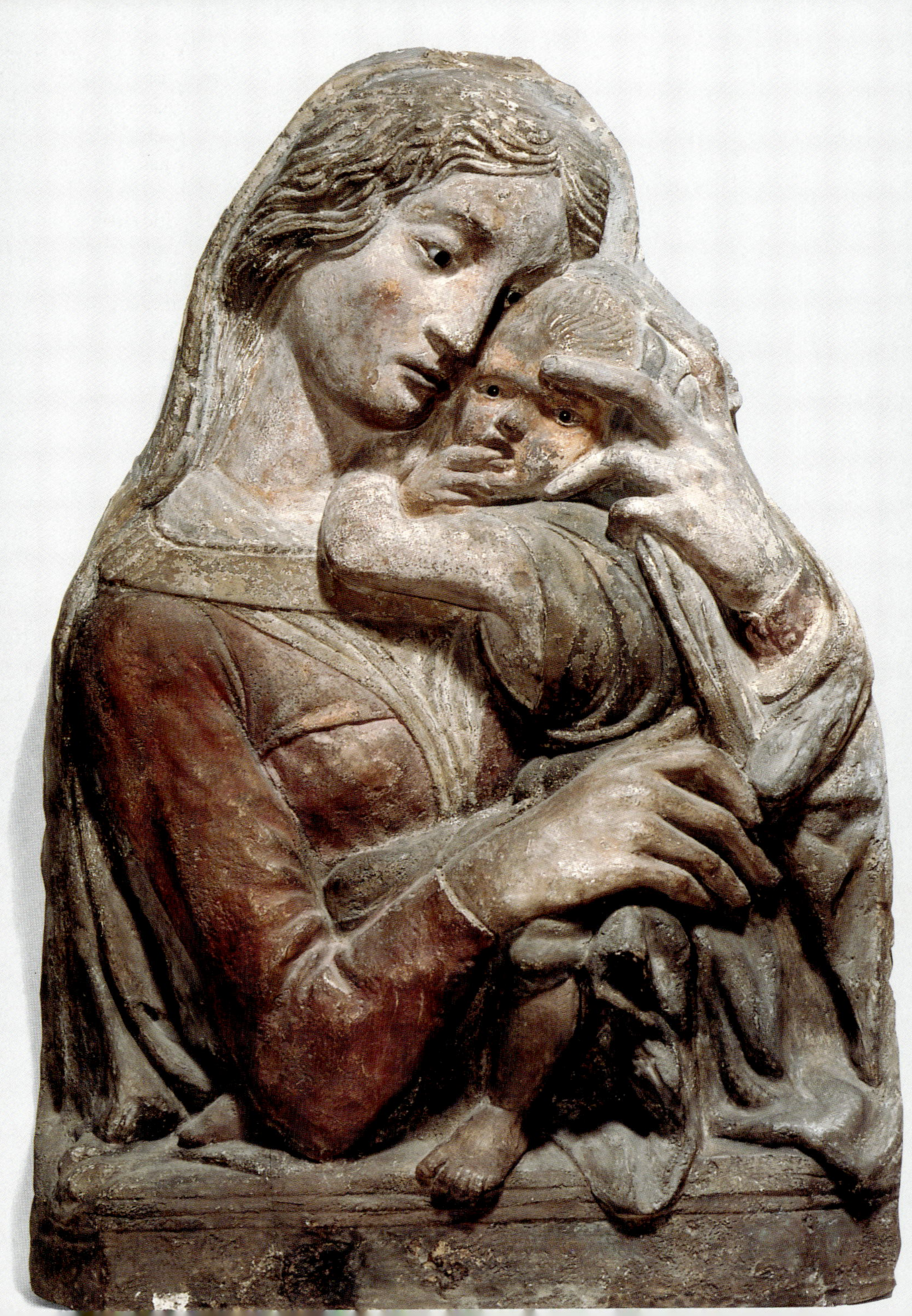

The Glorietta and the Sculpture Collection

Completely renovated in 1962, the seventeenth-century pavilion named the Glorietta is now the entrance to the gallery of Villa Favorita. Part of the original structure can be seen on the top floor, where the arches of a loggia offer a view of the entire lake. The most interesting decorative element of the building—in addition to the terraces adorned with stone *putti* and the motif of the arched windows which is found on each floor and lends formal harmony as well as conferring a feeling of lightness—is to be found in the building's interior. These are the three coffered ceilings that are visible in one of the rooms on the first floor and in two on the second. With their forthright Renaissance style, these testify to the taste for the historical period which prevailed at the turn of the century. Baron Thyssen-Bornemisza says that these were sent from Florence: it is certain that the only original is the one on the first floor above the area currently used as the gallery's bookstore. It probably came from Emilia and its decorative panels featuring classical profiles can be dated to the end of the fifteenth century [3].

The intention behind the installation of the works in the Glorietta is to illustrate the origins of the collection—its Old Masters—but also to present a broad panorama of the works, in this case sculpture, that the current Baron Thyssen-Bornemisza and his father have been interested in collecting. With notable exceptions—the series of ten *grisaille* panels painted during the eighteenth century by the Dutch painter *Jacob de Wit* (1695-1754) that depict the Evangelists and the Fathers of the Church, the interesting *Saint Francis* by *Bartolomé Esteban Murillo* (1618-1682) and another couple of seventeenth-century Dutch paintings—sculptures and reliefs in different media and from

**From a model
by Donatello**
*Madonna and
Child*, circa 1450

various periods dominate the stairs and the rooms leading to the actual gallery.

Although the assortment of works on display does not make tracing the history of the plastic arts through the ages possible, it does offer a chance to reflect on an often neglected theme, that of the materials used by sculptors, and to make some observations on the production techniques typical of Renaissance workshops.

When we look at a piece of sculpture, usually the first thing we wonder about is the subject. It is only later that we think about the date, the reasons behind the creation of the work, and maybe the genesis of its creative process. What we often forget is the essential element of the sculpture: the material. During the period that we discuss, which includes the works displayed (dated between the fourteenth and eighteenth centuries), sculpture was produced in a wide variety of materials ranging from marble, bronze, wood, gold, ivory, silver, and semi-precious stones, to terracotta and wax. The choice of a material was dictated by the work's function and meaning. This choice inevitably limited the work's eventual size, style and form. By definition, a marble statue or relief recalls the classical sculptural tradition. Marble is heavier than bronze and less ductile, making its extension into space more problematic. Unlike a sculptor using bronze, a sculptor working in marble could never make a statue of a horse resting on only three or two legs without having to insert a pilaster or rocks to support the statue.

Very few could realise monumental works in gold or silver. Nor was gold appropriate for more modest objects. Bronze was ideal for refined objects that were also easily reproduced. Some materials were more readily available than others (marble was more easily found in Italy than in Northern Europe); other variables included the form and the dimensions in which a material is found in nature (marble could be obtained in large blocks, but at great cost; jade came from faraway countries in extremely small pieces). The intrinsic characteristics of materials vary too. For example porphyry cannot be worked with metal tools; the colour of walnut is more uniform than that of oak; bronze reflects light; marble is cold to the touch; wood is less durable than other materials; terracotta is very fragile and tends to crumble when dry, and figures in terracotta weigh half again as much as those of the same size but made of another material etc.[4]

Throughout the medieval period, and especially in northern Europe during the following centuries, a wide variety of woods was used for figurative sculpture. Oak and walnut were typically used in

The Glorietta and the Sculpture Collection

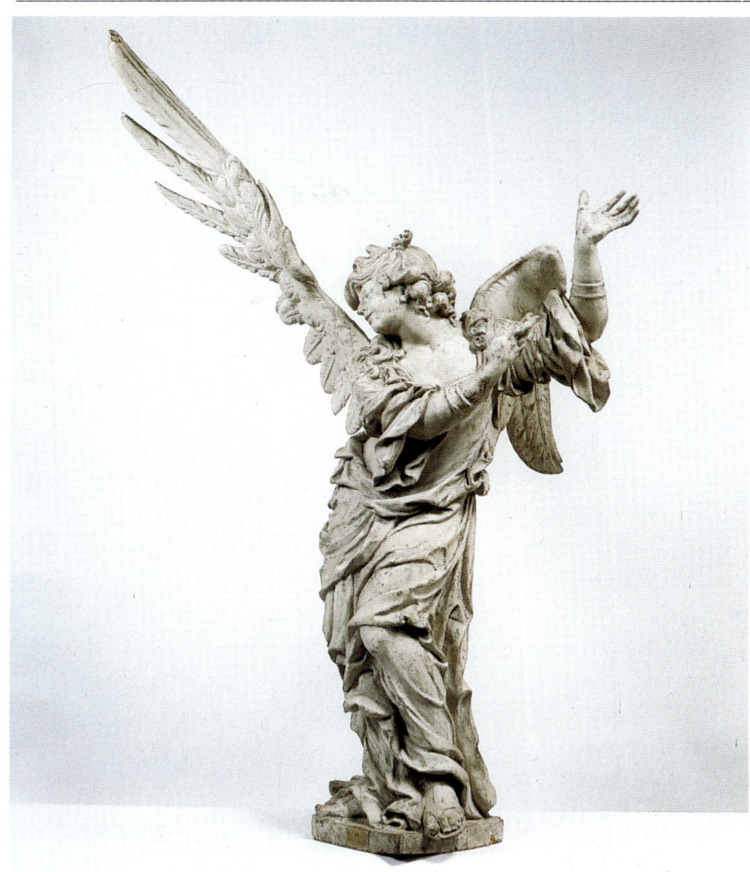

France and the Low Countries. Lime-wood prevailed in southern Germany, while pine and poplar were common in Italy and Spain. Because the properties of these woods—such as weight and density—vary so much, sculptors such as those who worked in southern Germany during the fifteenth and sixteenth centuries were able to produce works of a technical audacity unequalled by artists from other countries who had to use other types of wood. Even if wood is easier to work than stone, it still presents the sculptor with a series of problems. The greatest of these is that wood, as a result of the contraction caused by the loss of humidity, breaks and cracks after it has been carved. This problem can for the most part be overcome by eliminating all the superfluous parts of the wood that has not been sculpted, especially the central part of the log used in the work. The large medieval sculptures that have survived until today give us an oppor-

[4] An interesting study on the materials of sculpture is Penny 1993.

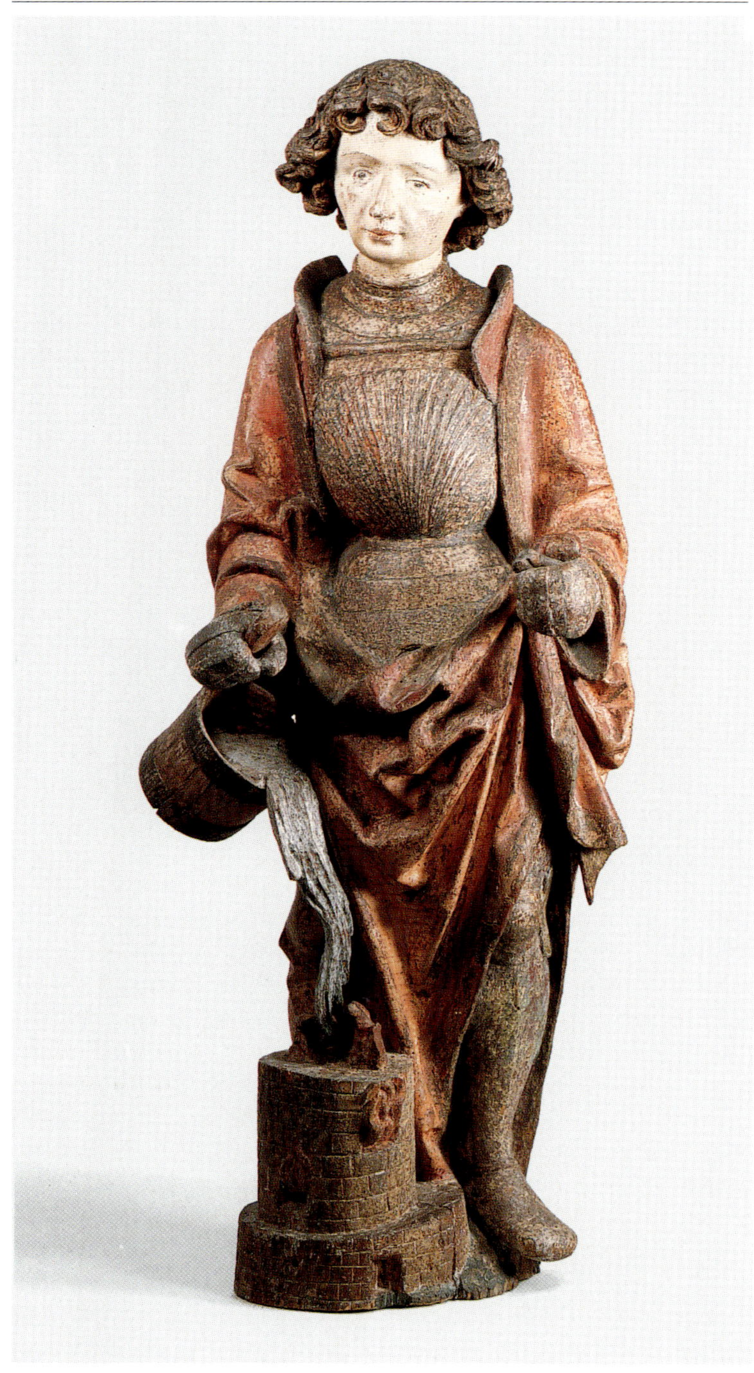

The Glorietta and the Sculpture Collection

tunity to observe how most of them were treated in this manner. It was more common for sculptures of wood than for those of stone to be painted and often further decorated with the application of other surface embellishments such as glass gems. Unlike stone sculptures, many wooden ones retain their polychromy and the original paint is probably still hidden under coats of paint of a later date. The intent was clearly to make these sculptures as realistic as possible.

Four of the sculptures displayed in the various rooms of the Glorietta are made of lime-wood and come from Austria and Germany. Lime-wood, as well as oak and walnut, was the most common type of wood used for European sculptures of large dimensions, particularly in Austria, Bavaria, Franconia and the area north of the Rhine. Lime-wood is relatively soft, light-coloured and elastic, and is not only easier to cut than walnut and oak, but is also less durable and less resistant to humidity. The two fine angels that the visitor encounters on the first flight of stairs are both of lime-wood and come from the workshop of *Michael Klahr* (1693-1743) an artist who was active in Silesia. These can be dated between 1725 and 1730, and are painted white in imitation of marble or plaster. Angels like these, depicted both kneeling and standing, usually flanked the altars of churches throughout central Europe. The complementary positions of the two angels and their somewhat rough workmanship on the back suggest that these too were made to adorn the two sides of an altar, in adoration of a painted image or a tabernacle. The thick folds of the cloth, the heavy curls and the round cheeks are all elements that point to contact with works influenced by Bernini.

Two works that are both from the early sixteenth century and from the area around Salzburg are a *St. Michael* and a *St. Florian*. The former—fully sculpted on only the front side, indicating that it was to have been mounted on a wall—represents the saint in a type of armour commonly found in southern Germany between 1480 and 1510. The second statue is stylistically close to works by Michael Pacher and was probably intended to "stand guard" over a small altar, more specifically on the right of such an altar, paired with a second guardian on the left. The small round base, the position of the tower in the foreground, its almost cylindrical form, the fact that both symbols can only be seen from the left side as well as the simplified treatment of the back in contrast to the rest of the figure all support this idea. St. Florian was a Roman soldier from Ems, in what is now the northern part of Austria. A convert to Christianity, he was martyred in 304 when he was thrown into a river with a millstone tied to his neck. He was found by some passers-by and it was said that an angel watched over his body until it could be buried. Tradition holds that St. Florian miraculously extinguished a fire with only the water contained in one bucket. For this reason, this saint who was very popular in Austria and Bavaria is typically portrayed, as in our case, near a city or house in flames and carrying a bucket.

The Thyssen collection contains two groups of statues in oak, which characteristically yields large logs, is very strong and resistant to humidity but is difficult to carve across the grain. The first group depicts *St. Anne, the Virgin and the Christ Child* and the second portrays *The Education of the Virgin*. The iconography of the latter is not found in the apocryphal written tradition of the life of Mary and its origins are unclear. This image was rather common in England in the first half of the fourteenth century, especially in Books of Hours and in alabaster sculpture groups. This work's style, which is reminiscent of several figures in the cloister of Notre-Dame in Paris, links it to the Ile de France. It can be dated to the mid-fourteenth century and is evidence of the rapid spread of this theme across the continent. The group portraying *St. Anne, the Virgin and the Christ Child* was made about a century and a half later in the southern Low Countries. The light colour that dominates the composition is clearly not original; instead it is the remains of the base layer of gesso under the polychromy, of which only a few traces are still visible. The apparent uniformity of this under-coat of gesso is the result of a more recent application of a coat of white paint. Despite its not particularly large size and the disappearance of its original base as well as St. Anne's throne, the group has a monumental and severe appearance. Even if they do not actually communicate with each other, the three figures, each with its own precise, individual characteristics, make a unified whole. St. Anne had been the patron saint of mothers, widows and single women since the twelfth century. In Holland and Germany, representations of this saint with the Virgin and Child became almost as popular as those of the Immaculate Conception, especially after 1481 when she was given a day in the ecclesiastical calendar.

A delicate bust of *Isabella d'Este*, attributed to *Gian Cristoforo Romano* (circa 1465-1512) and another of *St. John the Evangelist* by *Benedetto da Maiano* (1442-1497) are among the rare examples of Renaissance terracotta models for marble works that have survived until the present.

The sculpture of *St. John the Evangelist* is the model for a statue of the same subject on the marble altar in the Terranova (later Mastro-

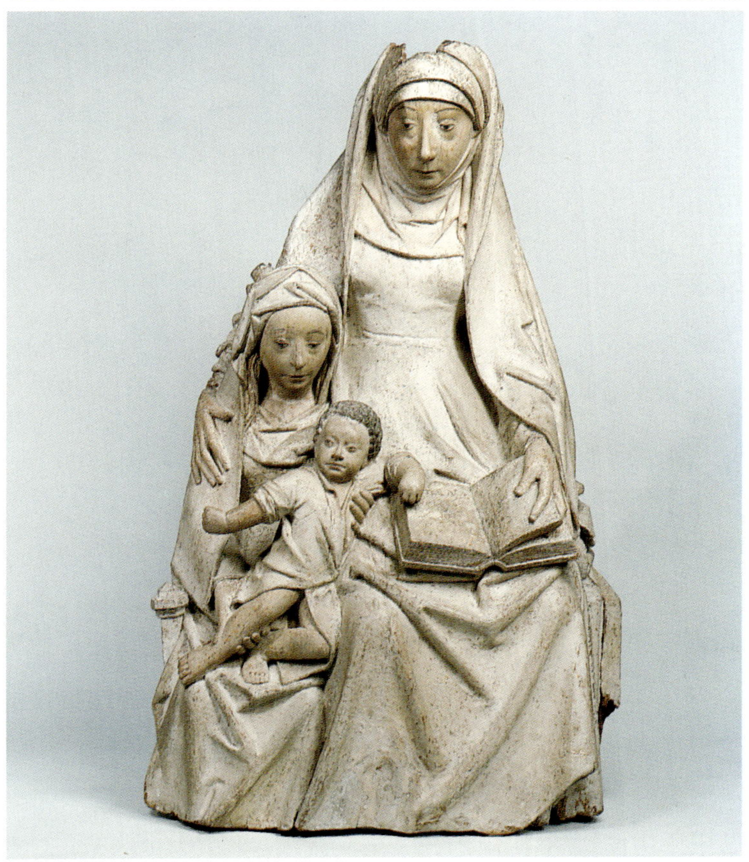

giacomo) chapel in the church of Sant'Anna dei Lombardi in Naples. The altar depicts the Annunciation and was completed by the Florentine Benedetto da Maiano and his workshop in 1489. It is one of the very few surviving terracotta models dating from the fifteenth century (it is not by chance that it was by Benedetto da Maiano, who had a very active workshop that produced not only marble statues, but also terracotta ones, including two others of an angel and God the Father for the Terranova altar). It is of some importance for the history of Renaissance sculpture as it offers a fine opportunity to deepen our knowledge of the creative process behind the production of a work in marble. In his treatise on sculpture (1568), Benvenuto Cellini (1500-1571) noted that it was common practice among sculptors to make small models in terracotta or wax. Regardless of the final work's actual dimension, artists worked directly from these without necessarily relying on other intermediate models. Artists considered these ancillary tools for their work or as models to present to a patron, and once their function was served they were put aside. Hence the rarity of these pieces. This *St. John* was most certainly executed with less attention to detail than would have been given to a completed work; its scope was merely to assist the artist; this can be easily seen from the way the clay has been worked. It is clear that Benedetto considered this model as something ephemeral to discard once its function was served: it owes its survival to the fact that it was still in his shop at his death in 1497 and was later sold to the abbot of San Frediano of Pisa to use on an altar in his church.

The first in chronological order of the three portrait busts made by Gian Cristoforo Romano—architect, sculptor, medallist and collector—is the marble one portraying Beatrice d'Este, wife of Ludovico Sforza. This bust certainly was the inspiration that led her elder sister to commission a similar one from the artist in 1491 and to buy the piece of marble for it. We know, however, that the sculptor did not arrive in Mantua until 1497, and there is no trace of a marble bust, which suggests that it was never made. The other two busts attributed to Gian Cristoforo portray Francesco II Gonzaga, Isabella's husband,

and Girolamo Andreasi Count of Ripalta. These are kept in the Palazzo Ducale of Mantua and the Bardini Museum in Florence, respectively. There is no doubt that the person the bust depicts is Isabella d'Este; her dress and hair style correspond closely to those in a well-known drawing in the Louvre by Leonardo da Vinci. That this bust is a highly idealised and complimentary rendering of the face of the sovereign of Mantua—who was not particularly beautiful though she was vain—is clear from Leonardo's drawing and other sources as well as in the contrast of the face with the naturalism of the shoulders and neck. We must not forget that this is a court portrait and that it was meant to give prestige to the person portrayed and to eliminate all her defects, if possible. We also know from historical sources that Isabella was a particularly difficult patron; she rejected a portrait of her done by the Mantuan artist Gian Francesco Maineri because she felt the likeness was too heavy. In contrast, she adored the portrait that Titian did of her at an advanced age as he based it on an earlier portrait of her when she was young (Kunsthistorisches Museum, Vienna). Before working on a portrait in marble, the artist usually prepared a life-size clay model of the person. He may have been aided by a direct cast of the face (a death mask in the case of a posthumous portrait) or he may have modelled free-hand assisted by precise measurements. It is probable that the bust of Isabella was made with these techniques.

There are only two marble works exhibited in the gallery. *Pietro Bracci* (1700-1773), one of the major figures in late-Baroque Roman sculpture and a passionate scholar of literature and philosophy, is the maker of the bust of *Pope Benedict XIII*. Among his public and private commissions is the famous group of *Neptune and the Tritons* that adorns the Trevi fountain. This bust, in which we can clearly see the sculptor's notable gift for portraiture, depicts Pope Benedict XIII Orsini-Gravina, of whom Bracci also left numerous other effigies and for whom he created the monument in Santa Maria sopra Minerva in Rome. The obvious differences in physiognomy and psychological characterisation between this image, in which the pope appears watchful and rather young, and others done by Bracci during his papacy (1724-30), where he is portrayed as ascetic as well as inept and disappointed (which indeed he truly was), indicate that this is a posthumous portrait. The difference with respect to the portrait done two centuries earlier by Gian Cristoforo Romano is enormous. The sitter's personal dignity remains untouched, but how much more attention has been given to revealing his "state of mind"! A second

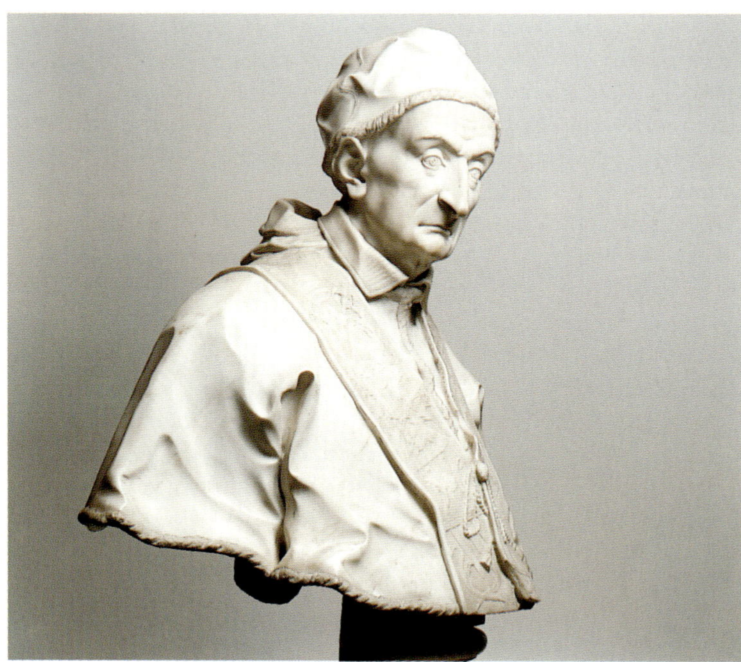

version of this work may be found in the Biblioteca Ambrosiana in Milan.

The second work in marble portrays a child seated on a pitcher. It was meant to be the central element of a fountain and to be seen from below. The child's back, which is perfectly perpendicular to the base, and the fact that the channel for the water is on the back rather than the bottom of the sculpture suggest that it was meant for a wall fountain, even if in this case the shell in the figure's right hand would be hidden from the viewer. Based on the stylistic and iconographic evidence, this figure seems to belong to a group of small *putti* realised around the mid-sixteenth century in Florence. These ornamental motifs for fountains were inspired by the *putti* of the Hercules fountain in the Medici villa at Castello and are the work of the Florentine *Niccolò Tribolo* (1500-1550).

Three reliefs depicting the Virgin and Child displayed on the ground floor offer an opportunity to make some observations regarding the production of multiples in the fifteenth century, in particular the Madonnas produced in plaster in Florence as well as those produced by the della Robbia workshop. The first of the three reliefs in question derives from a model by *Donatello* (1386-1466). It was made

The Glorietta and the Sculpture Collection

in a workshop in either Padua or Verona around the middle of the fifteenth century and is certainly the most interesting of the three. It can be seen to the right of the entrance of the Glorietta. This relief is in plaster with a few traces of polychromy and testifies to the notable manufacture of terracotta and plaster pieces that owe their style to Donatello's circle. In 1403, the Florentine writer Giovanni de Dominici recommended that parents have sacred images that their children could recognise in their houses. Above all he suggested images of the Christ Child; he thought representations of Jesus in the Madonna's arms particularly suitable. We must not be led to believe that he was advocating having art in the home, as much as he advocated having sacred images that could serve as moral examples for children[5]. It is equally clear, however, that his descriptions of images of the Virgin and Child refer to images that were already common in Florence at the time and that are recognisable in the plaster or terracotta reliefs manufactured by various Florentine artists during the first half of the fifteenth century, of which many examples have survived. The half-figure relief of the Madonna and Child destined for use in the home is a typically Florentine phenomenon. The earliest examples that have survived are in painted terracotta and come from the workshop of Lorenzo Ghiberti. Around 1420 Luca della Robbia produced a mould for a relief of the Virgin and Child with angels in a tondo. Many casts taken from this mould still exist. The use of moulds in his workshop seems to have increased during the last years of Luca della Robbia's career and was continued on an even larger scale by his grandson Andrea (an interesting example of a glazed terracotta relief is that depicting the *Madonna and Child with Angels*, from a model by Benedetto da Maiano, and a cornice from the workshop of the third della Robbia, *Giovanni* (1469-1529/30), which can be seen between the two windows by the entrance to the Glorietta). Donatello seems to have dedicated his energy to making this kind of relief around the 1430s, as is shown by a work in marble, known as the *Pazzi Madonna*, now in Berlin. He seems to have done the model of the Madonna that is more frequently reproduced, the *Verona Madonna*, about twenty years later, when he was in Padua. More than twenty versions of this have survived, including the one in the Thyssen collection. These could be made in many types of material, from *papier-mâché*—for domestic use—to plaster (like the one on display), and were probably intended to be placed on street corners as they often are in Florence.

Proof of the popularity of these reliefs, among twentieth-century

[5] See A. Radcliffe, in Radcliffe, Baker, Maek-Gerard 1993, pp. 16-23.

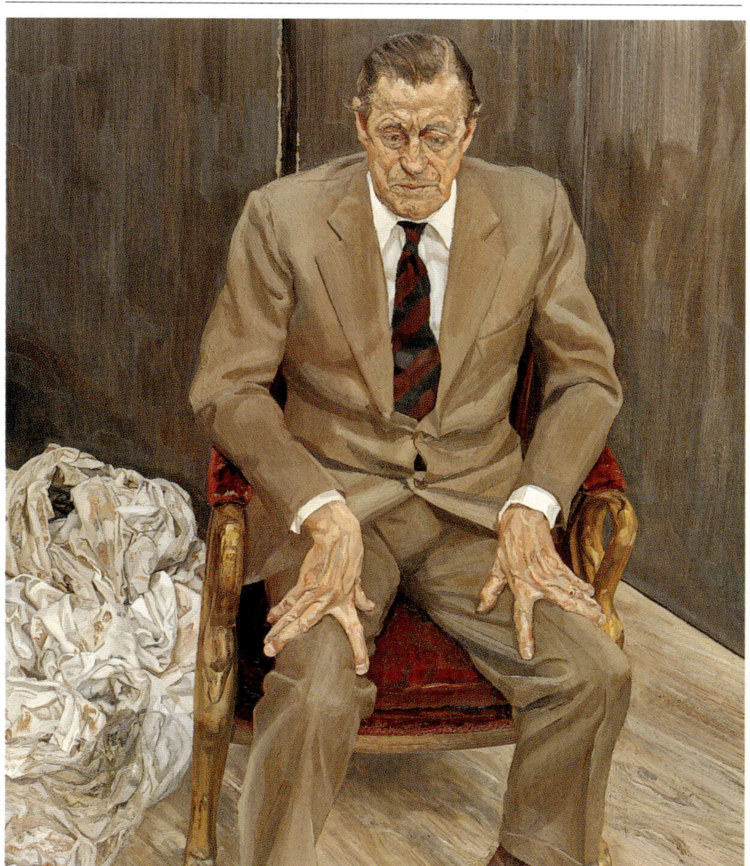

collectors as well, is found in the numerous copies—and deliberate forgeries found on the art market—in private collections and museums, particularly outside of Italy. The last of the three reliefs visible in the gallery is an example of the latter. Of marble, it is reminiscent of the manner of *Antonio Rossellino* (1427-1479) and was probably made in a Florentine workshop at the beginning of the twentieth century. The relief is overworked and there is an excessive interest in details. In addition, the presence of an architectural background, which never appears in works by Rossellino, and the absence of his delicacy and sense of style not only exclude the paternity of the Florentine artist, but also, according to Anthony Radcliffe in the catalogue of the collection's Renaissance sculpture, exclude the paternity of Giovanni Bastianini, the famous forger who "reproduced" many Renaissance reliefs

The Glorietta and the Sculpture Collection

with great sophistication in the 1850s and 1860s (Radcliffe 1992).

The last work that must be considered before we enter the gallery proper is an extraordinary painting by *Lucian Freud* (b. 1922) entitled *Seated Man*. This is a portrait of Baron Hans Heinrich Thyssen-Bornemisza, painted between 1983 and 1985. This portrait certainly will not seem flattering, even to a superficial observer. Nor are other portraits by Freud, because "the long hours of studio scrutiny, the 'ordeal' of sitting, of being watched and observed—often over months and years—lead to a unique confidence. Sitters become free to deliver themselves, unreservedly, into the artist's hands", London 1988). In "normal" portraiture, a tacit agreement between painter and subject allows the sitter to project his mask of success, dignity, beauty, role upon the world, as we have already seen in different forms in the two sculpted portraits we discussed earlier. In this case, the subject's face, with its downward glance and lowered eyelids, is captured in a moment suspended between inward reflection and outward expression, and is "as naked as a hand".

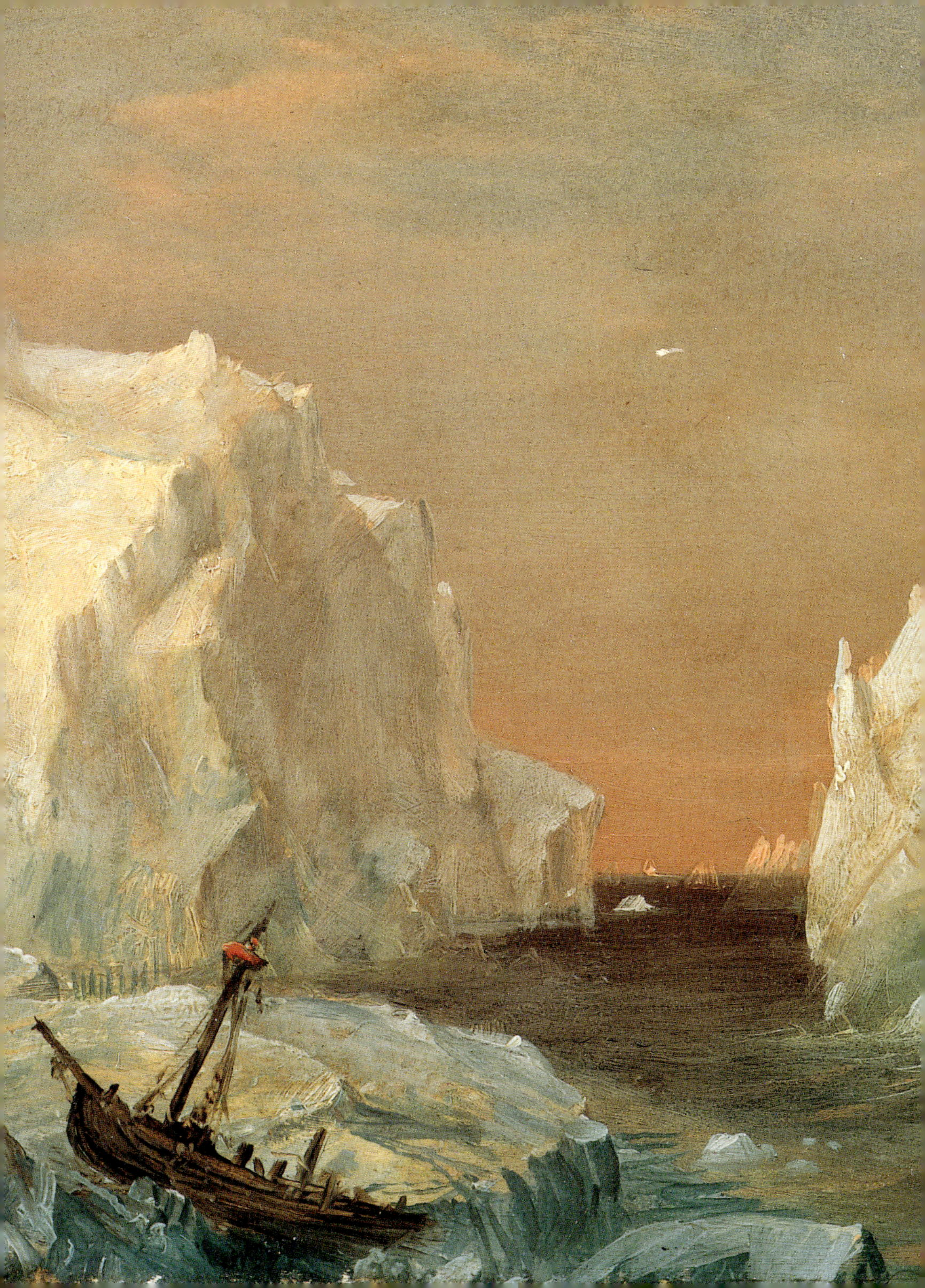

Nineteenth and Twentieth-Century American Painting

The Thyssen-Bornemisza Collection contains an important group of American paintings from the nineteenth and twentieth centuries. These paintings, acquired during the 1970s and 1980s by the current Baron Thyssen-Bornemisza, were not exhibited in the Villa Favorita gallery until 1992. They now form the nucleus of the collections discussed in this guide.

As Baron Thyssen-Bornemisza himself observed in the preface to an exhibition catalogue: "For a long time Europeans underestimated American art and considered it, with the exception of post-Second World War American art, as being inferior to European art. One must not forget that Van Gogh was not able to sell a painting during his lifetime, and had it not been for the Steins, the Morozows and the Shchukins, the Impressionists might be nowhere"[6]. Hans Heinrich Thyssen-Bornemisza was one of the first European collectors to become interested in nineteenth and twentieth-century American art. American painters had always attracted his attention, not only because he is one-quarter American himself, but also because of the great love of nature, open spaces and their land that distinguishes them.

The paintings in the collection make it possible to follow the main currents of American painting along these two centuries, from the search for an identity to the total independence from European art that eventually found its most complete expression in the works of artists after the Second World War. Only then did the flowering of Action Painting on the East Coast and the Informal school on the West Coast put an end to the relationship between the United States and Europe, which had always been characterised by the former's tacit acceptance of the latter's supremacy.

Frederick Edwin Church
Iceberg and Shipwreck at Sunset, circa 1860, detail

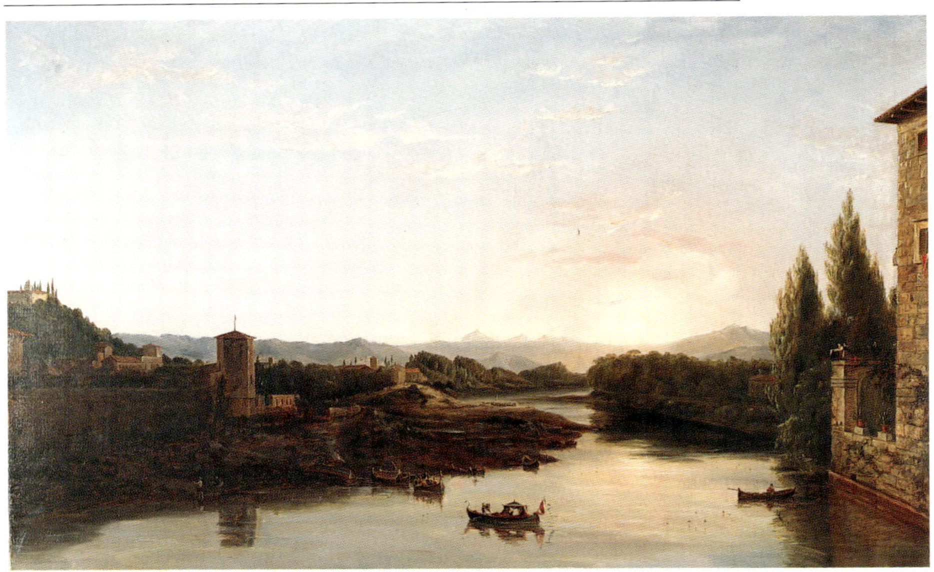

The Hudson River School

At the beginning of the nineteenth century, landscape was recognised as a theme suitable for representing the history of a nation that did not have much of a past to speak of.

The classical or Renaissance heroes whose deeds were considered the stuff of historical painting, which enjoyed a position at the top of the academic hierarchy in Europe, were out of place in America. Moreover, there were no academies in America, although eight-eenth-century connoisseurs had a clear conception of the subjects that were considered appropriate for painting. The theories of Sir Joshua Reynolds, *arbiter elegantiae* of eighteenth-century English society, who observed that painters such as Claude Lorrain or Willem van de Velde II— among the most admired landscape painters of the preceding century—deserved as much to be called painters as the authors of satirical or pastoral poems deserved to be called poets, were well enough known in American intellectual circles to influence patrons who had long preferred portraiture to other types of painting. The true history of American art begins with the "discovery" in 1825 of the work of Thomas Cole by three major New York artists (Asher B. Durand, John Trumbull and William Dunlap). Cole was subsequently "canonised" by the then mayor of New York Philip Hone, who in describing a picture of Cole's that he owned, publicly affirmed that "every American is bound to prove his love of country by admiring Cole"[7].

Thomas Cole
View of the Arno,
circa 1835-38

[7] Howat 1978, p. 29.

Nineteenth and Twentieth-Century American Painting

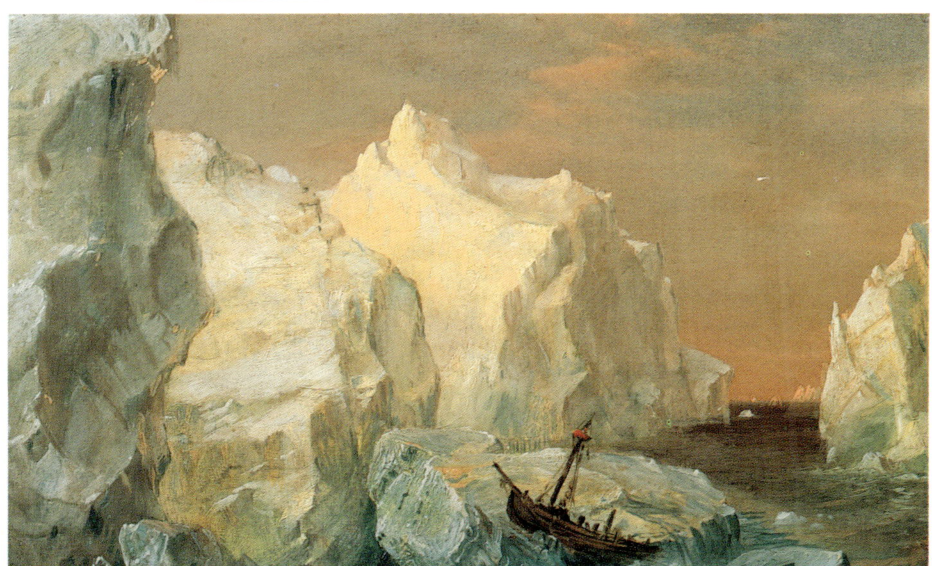

Interest in landscape painting and the resulting birth of the first movement of American landscape painting, known as the Hudson River School, were rooted in a specific, social, cultural and economic situation. For the first time in American history, life had become sufficiently comfortable for even the common man to regard the wild outdoors of the American continent as a natural marvel rather than as a threat. In their novels, James Fenimore Cooper and Washington Irving sang the virtues of rural life on the frontier; the philosopher Ralph Waldo Emerson and the writer Henry David Thoreau described a basic human need for solitude in the midst of the natural world, of whose purity even the common man was convinced. The artists of the Hudson River School belonged to this tradition: they were pantheists who believed that nature was created by God alone and was thus charged with a lofty and sacred meaning. They abandoned their studios to search for this meaning in the Catskill Mountains and along the Hudson River, even travelling as far as the White Mountains in New Hampshire, the coast of Maine and the great mountain ranges in the West. They saw the natural landscape as a direct manifestation of God and sought to record what they saw as accurately as possible with the reverence for nature of natural scientists. Unlike European landscape artists who repeated centuries-old styles and techniques in their canvasses, the Hudson River painters wanted neither to beautify nor idealise the scenes they depicted. When asked in 1847 what art was, a critic responded that art was the faithful imitation of nature. This declaration stood its ground throughout the greater part of the century.

Nevertheless, pictorial realism was neither the principal nor the only cultural reference point of the era. Over the course of the years, there grew a belief in the artist's right to interpret nature as an area for expressing a specific emotion. "Sublimity or awful grandeur, solitude, sweetness, cheerfulness, tenderness, fear, peace, love, melancholy... may all speak from the landscape unaided by human figures" as a critic wrote in 1856[8]. To achieve this result, nature was submitted to a manipulative process that went well beyond the confines of realism, even though it remained within the formal area of reality.

This is a general outline of the philosophy and methodology of the Hudson River School, which produced landscapes over a period of fifty years. These are characterised by a melodramatic approach, solid faith in the authenticity of religion and a fervent patriotism that saw America as an earthly paradise. These characteristics appear in the work of *Thomas Cole* (1801-1848) from the very beginning. His importance, and the importance of the school he founded, in their common devotion to the natural world, depicted in his paintings with a quiet and lyric realism, and the reconstruction of specific emotional states that he rendered with free melodramatic effects. The painting *View of the Arno* (1835-38), which the artist painted following a visit to Florence (it is worth noting that he did not execute the painting during his trip, but from memory on his return), while it does not represent an American landscape is still a perfect expression of Cole's theories. This is a real, but idealised, landscape; the representation of the American dream of Italy, "the Italy we dreamed of... of romance, poetry" as Cole himself wrote in a letter in 1832.

The same characteristics are found, perhaps expressed with even greater clarity, in the works of *Frederick Edwin Church* (1826-1900), Cole's only student. Church produced a series of landscapes in which the human figure appears tiny in comparison with immense mountain peaks or luxuriant vegetation. In his tireless search for exotic subjects and sublime inspiration, Church travelled from the Andes to Labrador, returning home with huge numbers of sketches and studies. In particular *Iceberg and Shipwreck at Sunset* is based on his various studies of the huge floating blocks of ice that he saw in Labrador. Between the 1850s and 1860s, Church was the most well-known American landscape painter, both at home and abroad. Church owes most of his far-flung fame to his large-scale landscapes. His particular

[8] John I.H. Baur, *Duecento anni di pittura americana dalla collezione Thyssen-Bornemisza,* in *Maestri americani...,* 1984, p. 16.

talent for realising detailed sketches was of great help when he executed these enormous landscapes as it allowed him to bring together an astounding quantity of minutiae in a vast panorama. Church achieved an encyclopaedic and stunning impact that fascinated and amazed the public. He did this by first eliminating the detail in the foreground and then accumulating it in the rest of the painting, where it had the effect of pushing the viewer right into the painting's interior. Inspired by von Humboldt's thirst for exploration and his own profound religious faith, he created his fantastic scenes in the belief that their large dimensions and his beloved detail would express his most profound ideas about man's intimate relationship with the grandeur of nature.

Asher B. Durand was another leading exponent of the same generation of artists as the Hudson River School; unfortunately none of his works are on display here.

The following generation produced artists such as Albert Bierstadt, Jasper F. Cropsey, Henry Lewis, William Louis Sonntag and Worthington Whittredge. The works of *Jasper Francis Cropsey* (1823-1900) in the gallery are particularly close in spirit to the works of Cole (for example *Ideal Landscape: Homage to Thomas Cole* and *View near Sherburne, Chenango County, New York*). More than any other American artist, *Albert Bierstadt* (1830-1902) expressed the sense of his country's grandeur through his representations of the uncontaminated outdoors of the Rocky Mountains, the Sierra Nevada and Yosemite Valley, which he visited repeatedly (for example *Landscape in Yosemite Valley*). While Cropsey, Cole and Church realised large and impressive landscapes of foreign scenes or America's East coast, Bierstadt depicted the wonders of the West coast on an epic scale. He could not have chosen a better moment than the years between 1860 and 1880, for at the same time the American and foreign press was much interested in the opening of the mountainous regions of the West, the real American frontier.

John Frederick Kensett (1816-1872) also belonged to the second generation of the Hudson River School. After travelling extensively in Italy, Germany, France, England and Switzerland, where he was able to study the great landscape artists of the past, particularly Claude Lorrain whose influence is visible in the compositional structure of many of his works (for example, *Landscape*, 1851), he returned to New York in 1847. In his search for mountains, woods, rivers and beaches he travelled widely from the Northeast to the Great Lakes and Colorado, producing hundreds of sketches and oil "portraits of rocks," as he described them. Kensett chose and painted what he saw and was not interested in allegorical or ideal compositions. Like Durand before him, he carried all his materials to his camps so as not to miss a single detail. He painted the quiet, serene and sometimes ordinary aspects of nature and was successful at majestically rendering the sun flashing on mossy, rough tree trunks deep in the woods (for example, *The Trout Fisherman*, 1852).

Sanford R. Gifford, Samuel Colman and David Johnson are some of the younger exponents of the Hudson River School.

The Luminists

If the painters of the Hudson River School used light to achieve melo-dramatic effects (for example Bierstadt's *Landscape in Yosemite Valley* or Cole's *View of the Arno*), other artists, known as the Luminists, made light the centre of attention and used it as a basic instrument for creating refined but unsentimental poetry about nature. This movement—technically not a movement since it did not espouse a specific structural theory—flowered between 1850 and 1875. Two painters were outstanding: Fitz Hugh Lane and *Martin Johnson Heade* (1819-1904). These artists decided to eliminate all evidence of their personalities from their paintings with the idea of ensuring that the poetry implicit in nature would be resplendent in their works, which are characterised by precise rendering of detail. To Lane we owe some

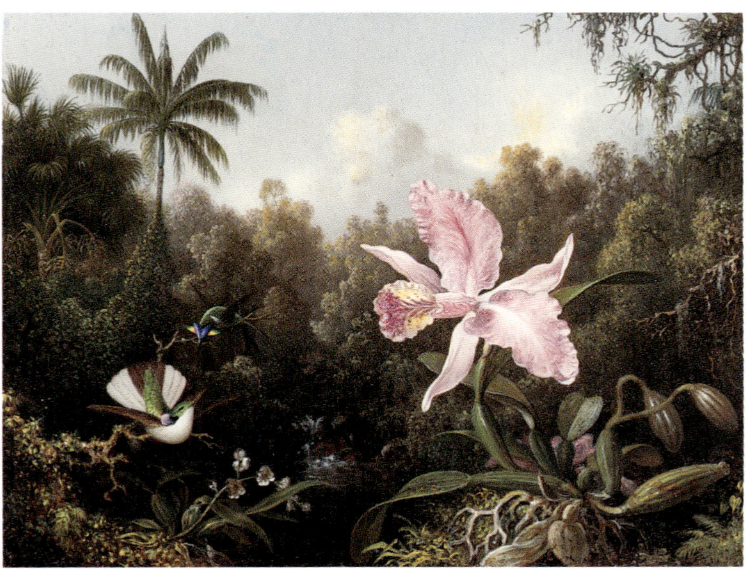

Martin Johnson Heade
Orchid and Two Hummingbirds,
1872

Nineteenth and Twentieth-Century American Painting

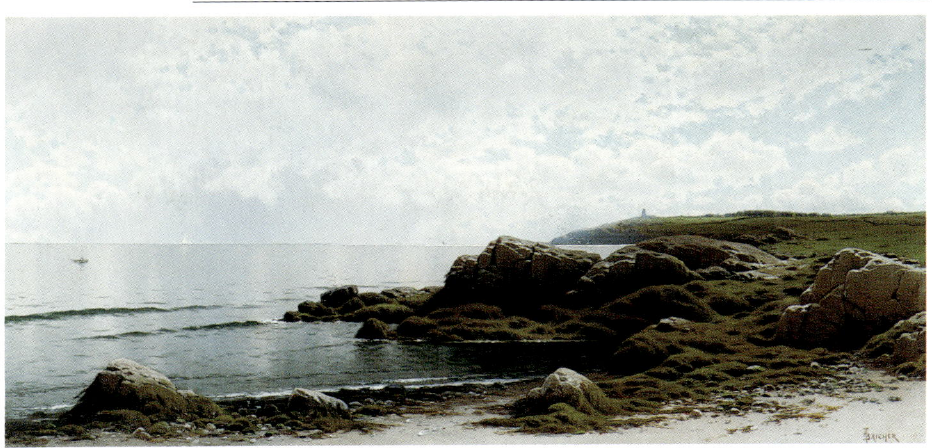

Alfred Thompson Bricher
Low Tide at Swallow Tail Cove, circa 1890-1900

of the most radiant panoramas of the New England coast, and to Heade unforgettable representations of the marshlands of New Jersey as well as of orchids and hummingbirds in tropical settings (*Orchid and Two Hummingbirds*, 1872). His trips to Brazil and Jamaica, which furnished him with pictorial material for a lifetime, were the source of the latter subject, which was certainly one of his favourites and earned him a special place in the history of American painting.

Even artists who are generally considered members of the Hudson River School such as *Sanford R. Gifford* (1823-1880), and *Samuel Colman* (1832-1920) executed works with a Luminist feeling such as *The Beach at Manchester* (1865) and *View of the Hudson River* (1865-69). Other less well-known, but no less important, artists such as *David Johnson* (1827-1908)—a master at rendering rocks and close-up views of tree trunks as well as large landscapes in the style of Kensett like the one exhibited in the gallery, *View of the Androscoggin River, Maine* (1869-70)—and *Alfred Thompson Bricher* (1837-1908) are also represented in the collection. The latter is worth noting for his *Low Tide at Swallow Tail Cove*, where every detail is meticulously recorded and incisively drawn, although nothing of the artist's emotions or personality is revealed. The cold, almost metallic light contributes to this sensation.

Painters of the Frontier

The works of the so-called frontier painters form another interesting part of the collection. While some artists went in search of the formal qualities that could be found in the American landscape, others undertook a careful exploration of daily life in its most various forms

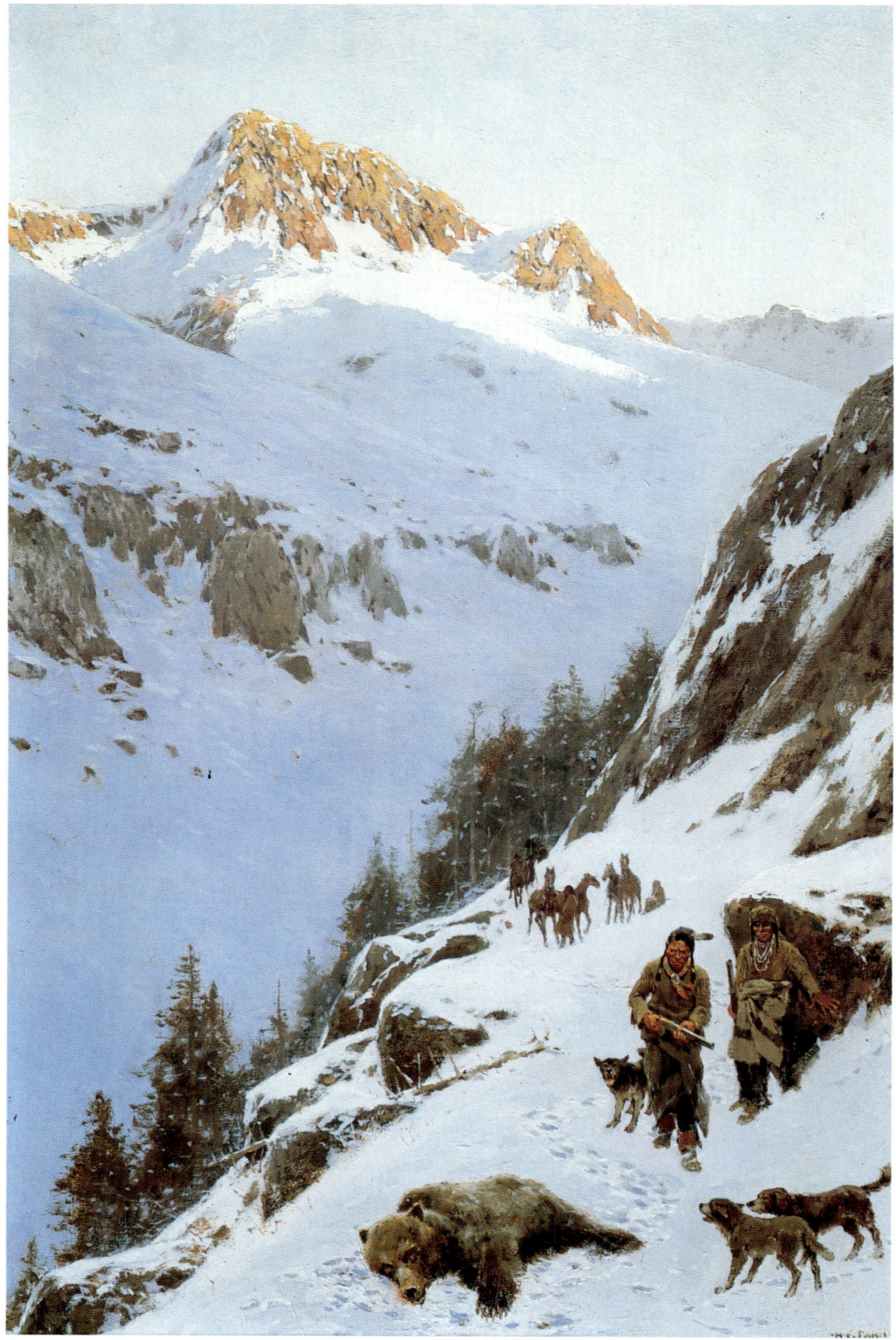

Nineteenth and Twentieth-Century American Painting

Henry Francis Farny

A Moment of Suspense, 1911

New Territory, 1893

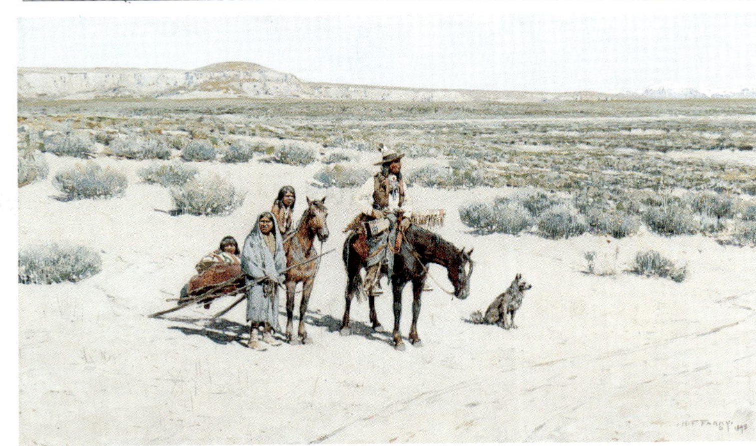

Frederic Remington
The Parley, circa 1903

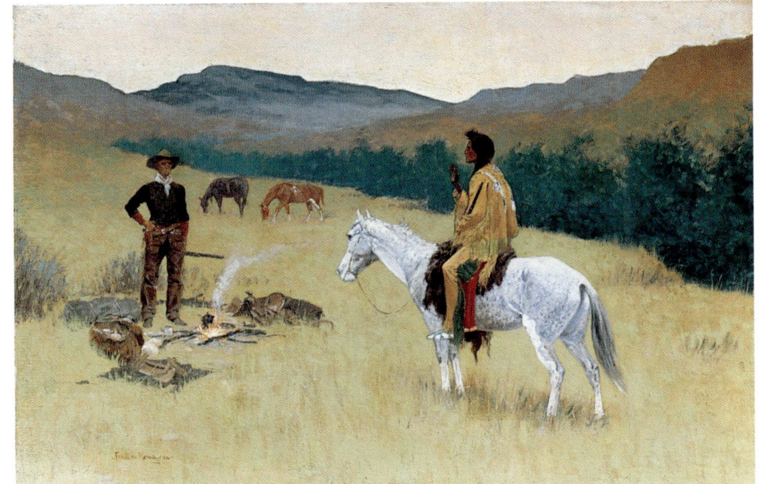

and in its most far-flung regions. The frontier painters, who were connected to this, were initially fascinated by the dangers of life in the West, but they soon became spokesmen for a world that was on its way to extinction. The territories of the American frontier still inhabited by Indians were the last to succumb to the "progress of civilisation" and became the subject not only of research expeditions but also of a rich literature and of countless paintings by artists of all levels of sophistication who were fascinated by the life and traditions of Native Americans.

Although Albert Bierstadt was the first to depict the grandeur of the unspoiled nature of the Rocky Mountains, the Sierra Nevada or Yosemite (as Thomas Moran after him), and though he more or less dictated the fashion for landscape painting for a long time, the most noted painter of the heroic epic of the American West is *Frederic Sackrider Remington* (1861-1909). Just as Bierstadt is the inventor of the Western landscape, Remington is likewise linked to the representation of the life of cowboys. His painting *The Parley* (circa 1903) is a good example. It must be remembered when viewing paintings such as this that for his contemporaries as well as later generations Remington's images provided indispensable and rich iconographic material suitable for whenever the West was to be depicted. In reality, what was being depicted was a world that had already disappeared and that came to life only in memories laced with Remington's own nostalgia for the West. He had lived and travelled in the West for many years and he believed it was the last rampart against the invasion of a way of life marked by technological progress and the European culture of America's big cities.

Henry Francis Farny (1847-1916), who studied in Munich and Düsseldorf, where he met Bierstadt, was another exponent of this "movement". His works are characterised by their realism and extreme precision of detail. They are based on the large quantity of sketches and photographs that he made during his numerous trips through the Rocky Mountains (*A Moment of Suspense*, 1911) and the State of Washington. The enthusiasm that came from his trips in the West led him to affirm that "the plains, the whole country and its people have more material for an artist than any European country". Nevertheless his works—like those of Remington—especially those painted in the 1890s, are the product of his imagination or studio reconstructions such as *New Territory* of 1893, where the precise details obscure the fundamental reality: by that date no new territory was being occupied by American Indians, because most of them had already been confined to reservations.

Nineteenth and Twentieth-Century American Painting

Impressionism

Towards the end of the nineteenth century, a profound change was taking place on the horizon of American art: the wide landscapes of the Hudson River School and the accurate realism of the Luminists were declared out of fashion.

The new pictorial directions of the final twenty years of the century were to be Tonalism and Impressionism.

Both movements rejected grandiose and faithful representations of reality; both tendencies preferred to suggest rather than describe. We can see this in paintings such as *Stream by the Farm* by *Ernest Lawson* (1873-1939) or *In the Garden* by *Theodore Robinson* (1852-1896). They are a long way, both stylistically and spiritually, from the artists whose works we have described above. American artists' contact with French art was fundamental for this change. The key year for the diffusion in America of the artistic innovations of the Impressionist movement was 1886. In April of that year, the French dealer Paul Durand-Ruel organised an exhibition of works by the leading Impressionist painters at the American Art Association in New York.

Until the end of the 1870s and the 1880s, the American public was only able to see contemporary European art rather sporadically. The decades of the middle of the century, as we have seen, were char-

Theodore Robinson
In the Garden,
circa 1891

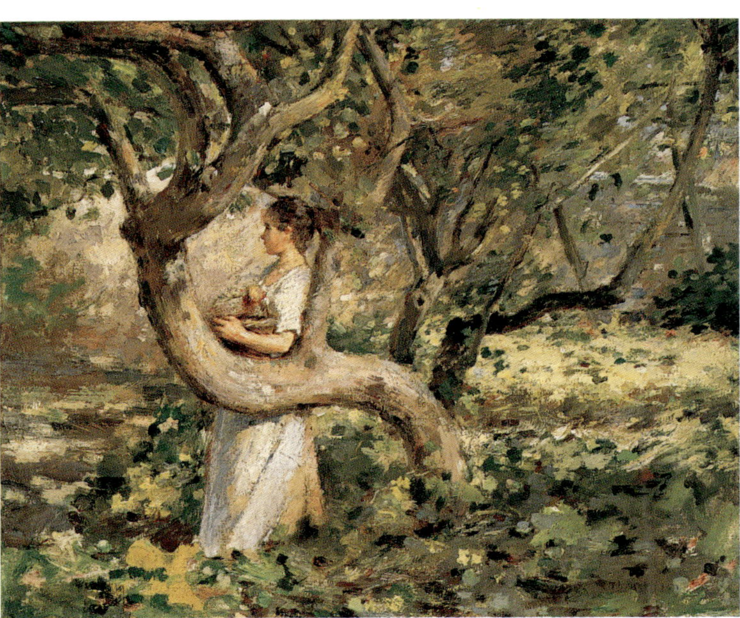

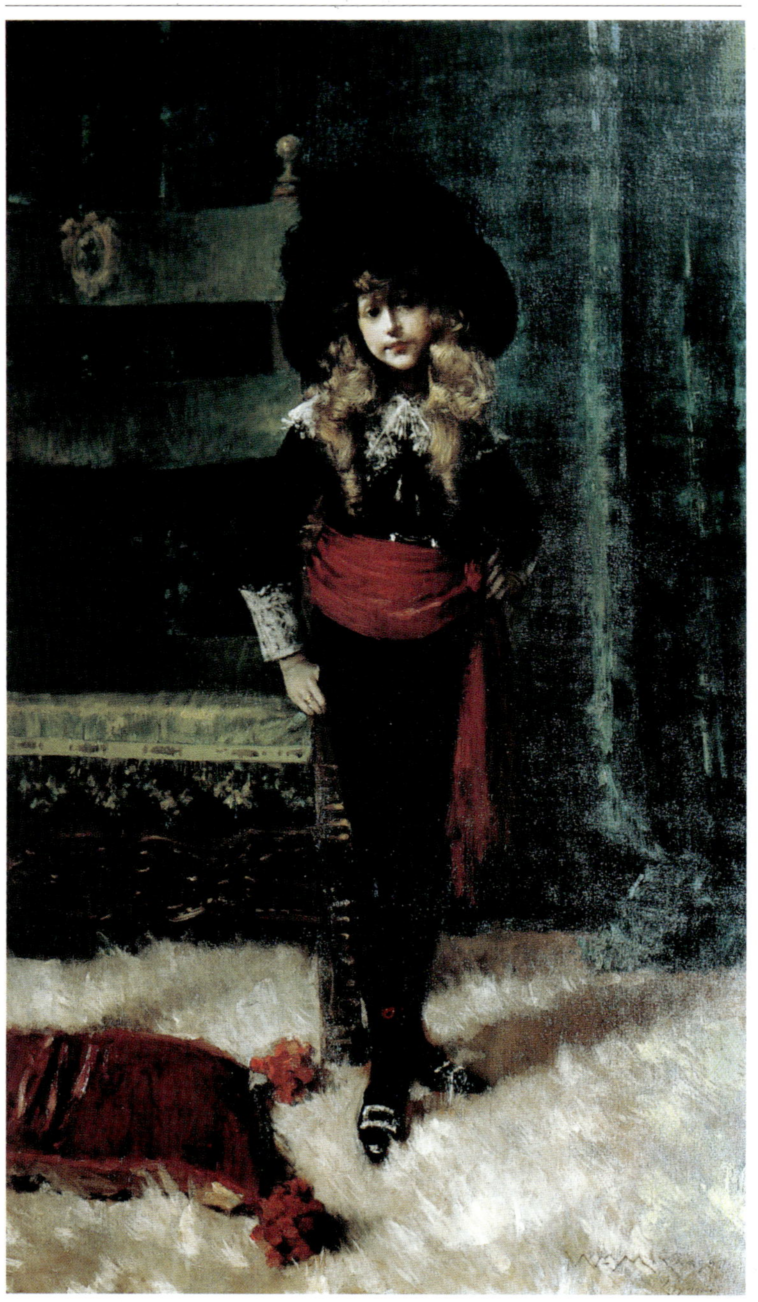

Nineteenth and Twentieth-Century American Painting

acterised by strong American nationalism and the celebration of the country itself. The comparison of the New World to the New Eden was defended by artists, writers and philosophers alike. However, at the same time many American painters also travelled in Europe and studied abroad: Germany, particularly Düsseldorf and Munich, was preferred to France. American artists tended to be rather suspicious of France and her artists. They admired the French conception of drawing, but considered the whole of French art violent and sensuous. In observing the works of these young artists who went to Europe, it is fundamental to remember that they did not go to the Old World in search of the avant-garde, but rather to learn the essential elements of traditional painting. The American students who were in Paris in the 1870s and 1880s did not go to bask in the influence of Manet or Degas, but to find an academic background.

Nevertheless, until 1886 most Americans were ignorant regarding the Impressionist painters. The American critics who were invited to the Durand-Ruel exhibition were stunned by the manner in which Manet and Degas rendered the human figure. Their writings bristled with words such as rough, unpleasant, gloomy or brutal. The landscapes were instead judged to be poetic, sensitive, joyous or fascinating. Therefore it comes as no surprise that when American artists began adopting the Impressionistic aesthetic they had a predilection for themes that were already dear to them: radiant children, ideal adolescents. They shunned the kind of scenes from modern life that attracted the French Impressionists: the street, cafés, and theatres. As we have seen, in the early nineteenth century, landscape was considered the theme *par excellence* of New World painters. While figure and history painting had begun to assume new importance for painters who had studied at the academies of Munich or Paris, Impressionism reaffirmed the primacy of the landscape. Thus it is not surprising that of all the painters present at the exhibition of 1886, Monet, landscape painter by definition, received the most praise and achieved the greatest success with American collectors in the following century. By 1887, a group of American followers of Monet had gathered around the French artist in the village of Giverny and in the years immediately following had already begun to send works to America and appear in exhibitions.

The first group to settle at Giverny consisted of six artists, including Theodore Robinson (1852-1896). He became a close friend of Monet's and was subsequently recognised as one of the most significant American Impressionists. Two of his works are displayed here:

On the Cliff (Girl Sewing) of 1887 and *In the Garden,* of 1891, which has already been mentioned.

In addition to Robinson, the principal exponents of Impressionism in America were Mary Cassatt, Childe Hassam, Henry Twachtman and Frederick C. Frieseke (none of whom have works in the Thyssen collection in Lugano), *Julian Alden Weir* (1852-1919), whose work *Silver Chalice with Roses* (1882) is reminiscent of works by Henri Fantin Latour, *William Merritt Chase* (1849-1916) and *Irving Ramsey Wiles* (1861-1948). The collection contains the large portrait of *Child Star Elsie Leslie Lyde as Little Lord Fauntleroy,* painted by Chase, the most fashionable portrait artist of the day, in 1889.

Urban Realism: The Eight or the Ashcan School

At the beginning of the twentieth century, American art was turned upside down by two revolutionary events: one regarding form, and the other regarding subject matter. The latter occurred first and involved a group of painters who called themselves The Eight or the Ashcan School. These young artists (Robert Henri, Ernest Lawson, Arthur Bowen Davies, Maurice Prendergast, Everett Shinn, William Glackens, John Sloan and George Luks)—some of whom had become known as newspaper artists serving their artistic apprenticeships while drawing on the street—claimed that art's subjects should come from the streets, parks and rundown areas of the city. This put them in conflict with the widely held belief that joy was the substance of life, and thus of art. From a stylistic point of view, none of the artists in The Eight was a true revolutionary (for example the painting by *Robert Henri* (1865-1929), *Marjorie Reclining* (1918), is rather close to works by William Merritt Chase), but they were successful in introducing a new vitality onto the American art scene and in laying the foundation for a new generation of painters who were interested in the life of the common man in New York.

The social realism of the 1930s is represented in the collection by artists such as *Ben Shahn* (1898-1969), *Thomas Hart Benton* (1889-1975) and *Edward Hopper* (1882-1967), who used the possibilities of Expressionism to develop narratives, often with a moral about the working class and its suffering (see Shahn's *Riot on Carol Street* and Benton's *The City (New York Scene)*. Isolation seems to be the dominant theme of Hopper, who was an artist profound enough to transform the sense of solitude and alienation felt by many Americans into a theme with universal meaning. His solitary clerks, elderly couples and deserted depots treated the depressing ordinariness of

Nineteenth and Twentieth-Century American Painting

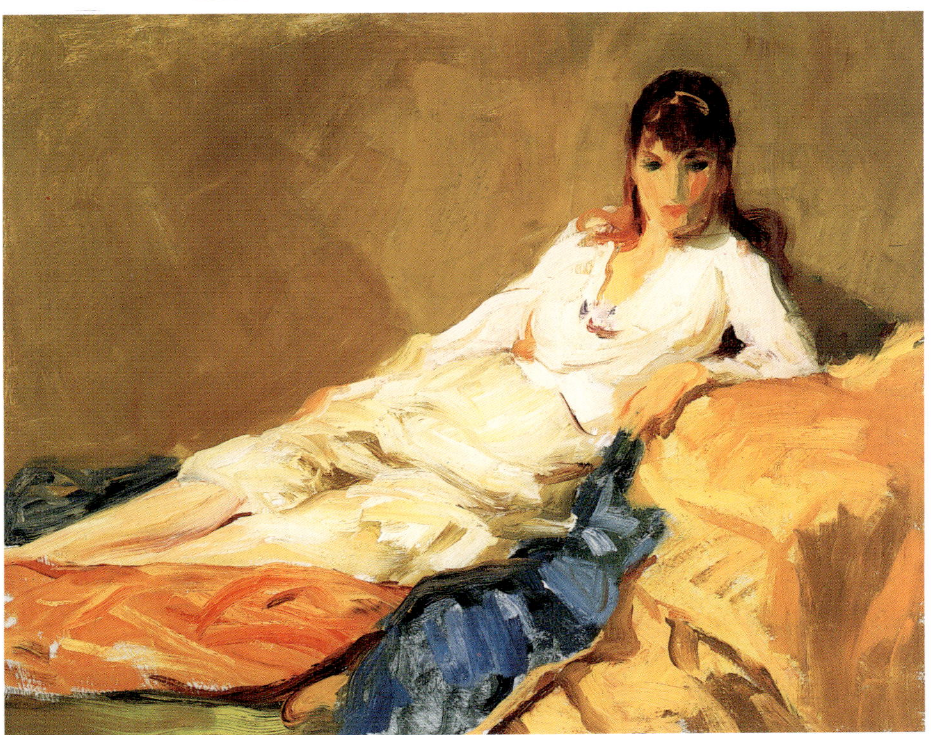

the democratic experience with a bitterness and compassion that enlarged their subjects to dimensions that transcended the small disappointments of daily life.

Thomas Hart Benton, however, with his total rejection of foreign influences, his populism and isolationist nationalism became the hero of anyone who wished to return to the good old days when America was a rural society, uninterested in creating an international style or participating in world affairs (in the gallery we may see *Pop and the Boys* of 1963).

The artist who more than any other seems to have inherited the concerns of the Ashcan School, particularly the teeming streets of New York, was *Reginald Marsh* (1898-1954), who favoured the depiction of street life over any other subject and captured its spirit wherever he found it (*Food Store - The Death of Dillinger* of 1938).

Early Modernism

The second revolution that took place in American art at the begin-

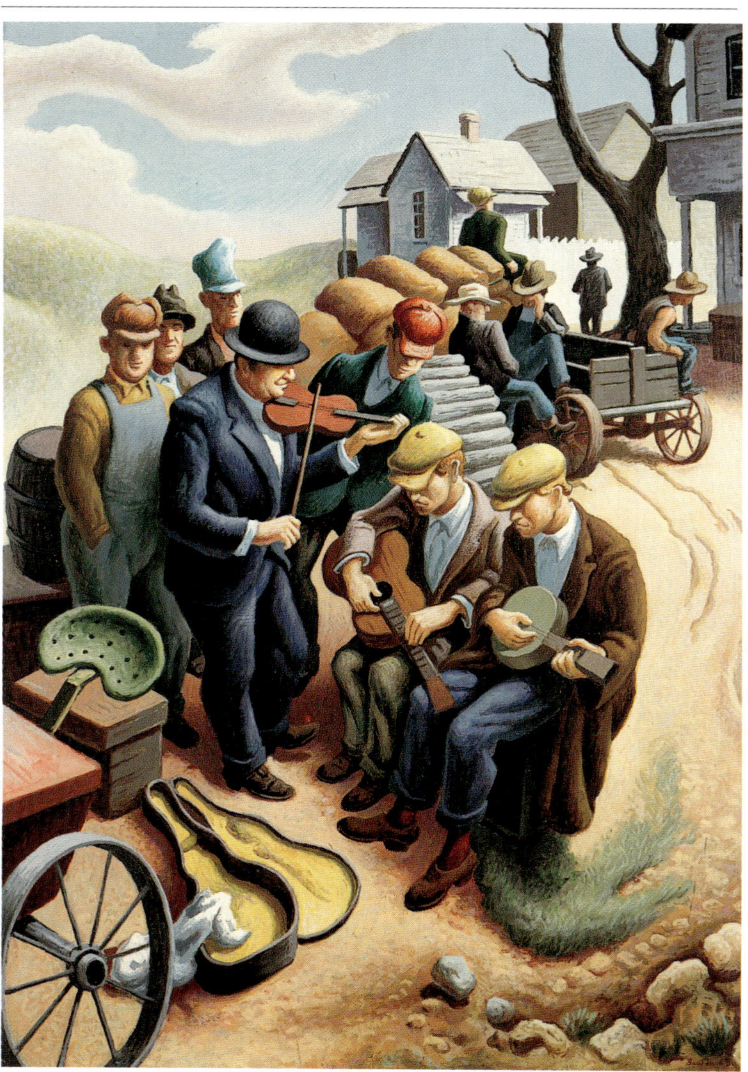

Nineteenth and Twentieth-Century American Painting

ning of the twentieth century concerned the formal revolution of Modernism. This was composed of two principal tendencies: Abstraction, which was based on the theory that the essential element of any artistic expression is pure form, and Expressionism, which was characterised more often than not by a violent distortion of form whose scope was to express equally violent emotions. Even if these two movements, both born in Europe, did not achieve wide popularity on American soil until the so-called Armory Show of 1913, American artists abroad played an active part in the diffusion of these two currents of contemporary art.

Two important groups of American artists showed their works at the Armory Show, the exhibition of modern art held at the armory of the 69th Regiment of New York, where a large number of both American and European artists active from the mid-nineteenth to the early twentieth century appeared before the American public for the first time. These were the Ashcan School and another group known as 291, from the name of the gallery on Fifth Avenue where they assembled. Robert Henri was the spokesman for the Ashcan School and we have already seen how he espoused a realism that was objective (even if "realism is relative") insofar as it was not based on a careful study of human anatomy or the traditional canons of painting but on journalistic illustration.

The intentions and works of the artists who gathered around the photographic genius Alfred Stieglitz at the 291 Gallery were rather different. For years Stieglitz had shown modern European art, and these works with their intense, direct expression of the idea that art itself represents a strong spiritual reality as relevant and meaningful as the material world, had an enormous influence on the artists of the 291 Gallery. These were the first American modernists. We must not be led to believe however that their only source of inspiration was European art; they also sought inspiration outside the fine arts, in folk and applied art. While the members of the Ashcan School expressed their observations of reality in an art that was primarily urban in subject matter, the group around Stieglitz drifted away from puritanism and looked towards another American tradition, the transcendentalist philosophy of Emerson and Thoreau. They sought to capture the sensual heart of life as it was manifested in nature and found their subjects not in the external world, but in their own interior—in their dreams and imagination—from which each developed his own vision of the American landscape. For American artists, heroic themes could not be tied to an anthropomorphic humanism based on classical or

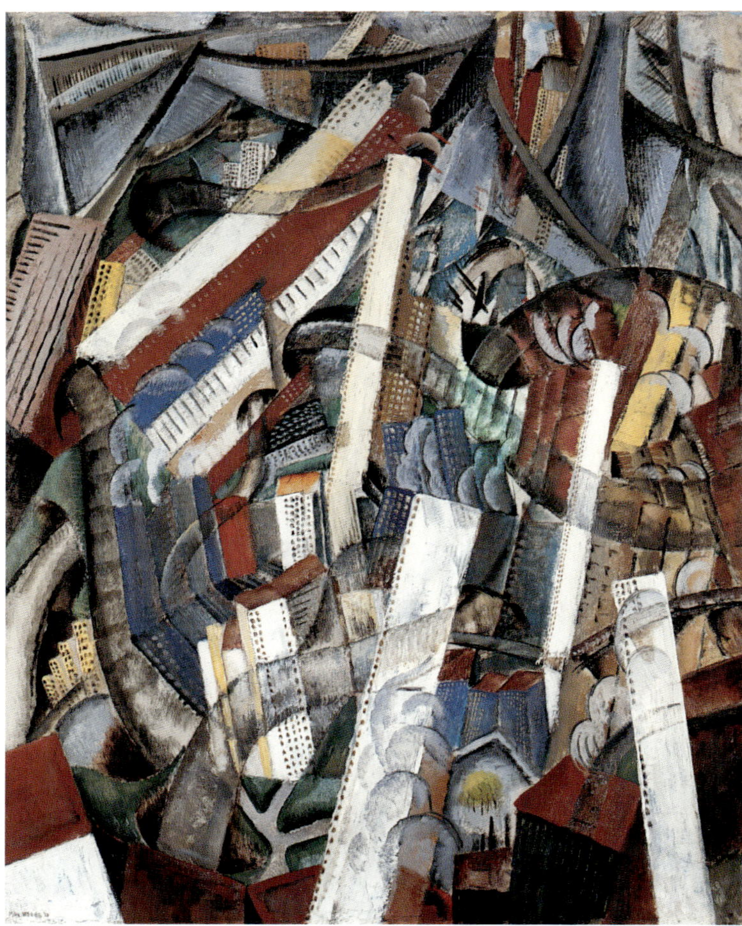

Renaissance subjects. The only relevant heroic subject for an American artist was, and continued to be, the epic grandeur of the American landscape. Even when American art came to its full flowering in the work of the Abstract Expressionists, these images did not evoke figures or the Cubist's still lifes, but the sublime power of nature.

Nevertheless, many American artists understood that their tradition was not strong or solid enough to continue to build and develop without any stimulation from outside. Thus a few began to study artists such as Picasso and Braque, just as the painters of the "American scene" had studied the Old Masters in their efforts to emulate their style and technique. In both these efforts it is important to see how they were actually only a strong reaction to their shared aware-

Nineteenth and Twentieth-Century American Painting

ness of how inadequate the American tradition was for creating a monumental style in the grand manner of the European tradition. Their aspiration for a heroic style capable of rivalling the ambitions and exploits of the finest art of Europe should be seen as the common denominator among this varied group of artists who worked during the period of America's Great Depression. This aspiration is perhaps the single most important and persistent characteristic that distinguishes the American artists of the 1930s from artists working at the turn of the century, who devoted themselves to intimate themes rather than to the creation of a public style. The moment for a mature American art ready to take its place among the great artistic movements was at hand.

Max Weber (1881-1961), who had studied in Paris and later became part of Stieglitz' circle when he returned to New York, was the first to move in this direction. Cubism rather than Impressionism was the style that he brought back with him. A good example of this is his painting of 1913 entitled *New York*, which is constructed according to Cubist and Futurist canons.

Another faithful member of Stieglitz' group was *John Marin* (1870-1953). The Thyssen collection contains two watercolours from the so-called *New York Series* of 1927; Marin's reaction to Cubism can be seen in their angular forms.

In the years following the Armory Show, the most articulate spokesman of American abstract art was *Stuart Davis* (1894-1964). In the catalogue of the 1935 exhibition of abstract art at the Whitney Museum, Davis wrote that art cannot be a mirror reflecting nature, and that all efforts dedicated to imitating nature are destined to fail. Moreover, abstract artists do not seek to reproduce what is unreproducible. Instead, their goal is to give material palpability to their means of expression, whose result will be the permanent expression of an idea or emotion inspired by nature. According to Davis, the most important question to ask of a painting is: "Does this painting, which is a defined two-dimensional surface, convey to me a direct emotional or ideological stimulus?". How different from what art critics wrote in the mid-nineteenth century!

Precisionism

In the 1930s, a group of artists who called themselves the Precisionists promoted another form of realism that attempted to combine abstraction and realism. The precursor of this movement was *Guy Pène du Bois* (1884-1958), who combined the social realism of The

Eight with an elevated simplicity capable of reducing both the human figure and the setting to the most generalized pictorial form. We can see this characteristic in the painting *42nd Street*—with its elegant women walking in Manhattan with the impersonal expressions and blank features of wax mannequins—or in *Le Viol*. Oscar Julius Blümner (1867-1938) succeeded in obtaining the same effect in his landscapes even if he placed greater emphasis on the expressive power of colour (see his *Red and White* or *Red Against Blue*).

The goal of the Precisionists (Charles Demuth and Charles Sheeler also belonged to this group) was to reduce and simplify form rather than to analyse it. They were among the first artists to realise that in America the European grand manner of painting was limited to producing rhetorical and empty art. To remain faithful to their experience, they felt a duty to put aside all pretence to grandiosity, to paint in a modest style and to chose ordinary, day-to-day themes. Like the Pop artists who followed them, the Precisionists painted humble subjects from everyday life or industrial machinery: see, for example, *Charles Sheeler*'s (1883-1965) *Ore into Iron*. The choice of such themes was also linked to the fact that for several decades after the Armory Show, American artists still suffered from a cultural inferiority complex with respect to their European counterparts. Thus they believed that to make an authentic and individual statement American art needed to limit itself to depicting the most ordinary forms and humble themes because these were characteristic of the American experience.

Late Modernism

After 1940, interest in abstract art, which had waned noticeably during the 1930s, returned as one of the principal issues that interested American artists. Some artists remained active supporters of pure abstract art, while others such as *Milton Clark Avery* (1885-1965) adapted the semi-abstract vocabularies of Cubism and Fauvism to the demands of other situations. Avery's lyric vision and exquisite sense of colour (see *Homework*, 1946) brought a new kind of poetry to abstract painting. Likewise, Expressionism maintained a good number of followers, including *Walt Kuhn* (1877-1949), who gave life to a sober representation of circus artists, characterised by his use of colour applied with heavy brushstrokes (*Chorus Captain*, 1935). However, it was *Charles Ephraim Burchfield* (1893-1967) who, towards the middle of the century, developed the form of American expression that was both the most original and least dependent on

European models. His friend Edward Hopper wrote of his art, "from the boredom of everyday existence in a provincial community he has extracted a quality that we may call poetic, romantic, lyric". Burchfield was first and foremost a landscape painter whose fantastic exaggerations often make him seem to be an Expressionist. Like Benton, he lived in the Midwest, but unlike Benton who sought to recreate the myths of rural American life, Burchfield created artworks that were more introverted, based on his private obsessions and fantasies about nature's disturbing powers.

Abstract Expressionism

The 1940s witnessed the arrival of a new artistic current that was destined to profoundly condition the development of American art during the following twenty years: Abstract Expressionism. This movement changed the character of abstraction from a style that was ordered, intellectual and classical like the work of the Cubists, into something intuitive, romantic and anti-aesthetic. The key of what was going to be called "Action Painting"—one of the currents of Abstract Expressionism—was *Jackson Pollock* (1912-1956). Action Painting was based on the suspension, at least in theoretical terms, of aesthetic judgement and on an openness to the most basic impulses exercised by the automatic and spontaneous responses of the hand in the act of distributing paint—with or without a brush—on the canvas.

A fundamental contribution to the growth of Abstract Expressionism came from Peggy Guggenheim, an American who had returned from Europe with her collection of Cubist, Futurist, Surrealist and Constructivist paintings, who opened her gallery Art of This Century in 1942. This gallery, like the Armory Show and 291 Gallery before it, became a new meeting point for American and European artists. The European artists who showed their works here and who had the greatest impact on the American colleagues were Kandinsky, Miró, Klee, Arp and Masson. In the 1930s, as we have already noted, American abstract painters were influenced by the strictly geometric abstractions of the Futurists and Constructivists and by the angular forms of synthetic Cubism, especially Picasso's.

These "classic" styles with their formal constraints, their closed forms and shallow, precisely limited space did not satisfy the American appetite either for showy expression, sense of physical presence and movement, or for intense, romantic imagination. The freely improvised drawing and ambiguous open spaces of Klee, Kandinsky and Miró gave American artists examples of styles that were more

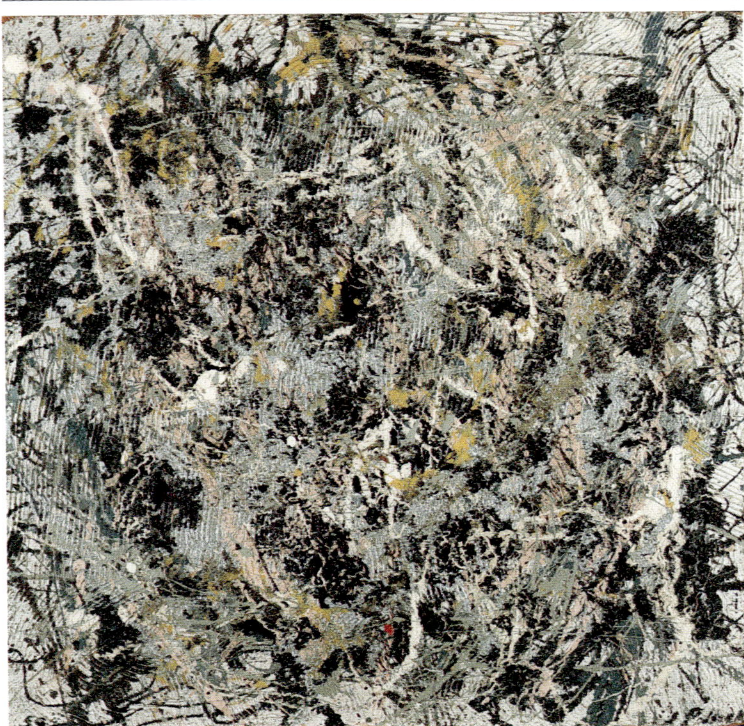

free and more to their taste for individual expression and yearning for romantic gesture.

The necessity of creating a new style coherent with these recent arrivals stimulated many New York artists to undertake a series of innovative moves that exploded into a chain reaction during the extraordinary decade of the 1940s. Notions of decorum and academic formulae were abandoned once and for all; any tool for painting was valid, as long as it could serve its purpose. Artists pragmatically appropriated instruments and materials that had never been used to make works of art before. Franz Kline found that house painters' brushes were excellent for creating large swathes of paint and inspired Frank Stella to use the same tool for his paintings of stripes. Adolph Gottlieb used a sponge mop for distributing large areas of colour in an impersonal manner. For his part, Pollock took these approaches to their extreme and invented a technique that consisted of pouring and throwing paint and eliminating all the conventional painter's tools. Between 1947 and 1951, his exclusive use of the drip technique created a homogenous surface that compressed drawing and painting into a single technique and eliminated the gap that had separated them until the arrival of Pollock. Now painting strove to reduce itself to its essentials, to distil its own essence. Pollock broke the ice for his fellow artists when he united painting and drawing into an automatic technique that no longer recorded the small, intimate movements of the hand but the grand, physical gestures of the wrist and arm.

The Thyssen collection contains three works by Jackson Pollock; two from the mid 1940s and one from 1950. The gallery also displays a work by Pollock's wife *Lee Krasner* (1912-1984)—*Red, White, Blue, Yellow, Black,* 1939—as well as her great friend *Alfonso Angel Ossorio* (b. 1916), whose work *The Cross in the Garden* of 1950 is similar to works by Pollock.

Photo-Realism and Hyper-Realism

The terms photo-realism and hyper-realism or super-realism apply not to a movement, but to a style that had a certain following in the United States in the 1970s. The point of departure was a combination of photography and technology that were used to create extremely precise pictorial reproductions of the urban landscape, cars, motorcycles and advertising. Although the use of these day-to-day images is similar to Pop Art, this is the only point that the two styles have in common.

Richard Estes (b. 1936) chose New York as his source of inspiration. Estes has observed that photo-realism is an abstract manner of seeing things without personal involvement, which is paradoxically similar to the style of the abstract artists. The only painting by Estes in the collection is *Hotel Lucerne* (1976). Another important exponent of this style is *David Parrish* (b. 1939), whose work *Three Yamahas* of 1976 is one of the most recent in the collection; we would like to end our brief history of two centuries of American painting with a work by *Richard Lindner* (1901-1978) entitled *Out of Towners* (1968).

Richard Lindner was hailed as a precursor of Pop Art in the 1960s. In reality, a German who had fled from Nazi oppression, after having worked as an advertising illustrator, he created a group of bold and difficult works that were completely estranged from the avant-garde tendencies of the time. Based on his personal memories and his emigrant's cultural heritage, Lindner created images of a bizarre and sinister humanity. His paintings of grotesque children, pairs of robots and inhabitants of the suburban world speak of the alienation and moral crisis of the twentieth century. Lindner's identity as a refugee artist helps us to understand his figurative symbolism, which origi-

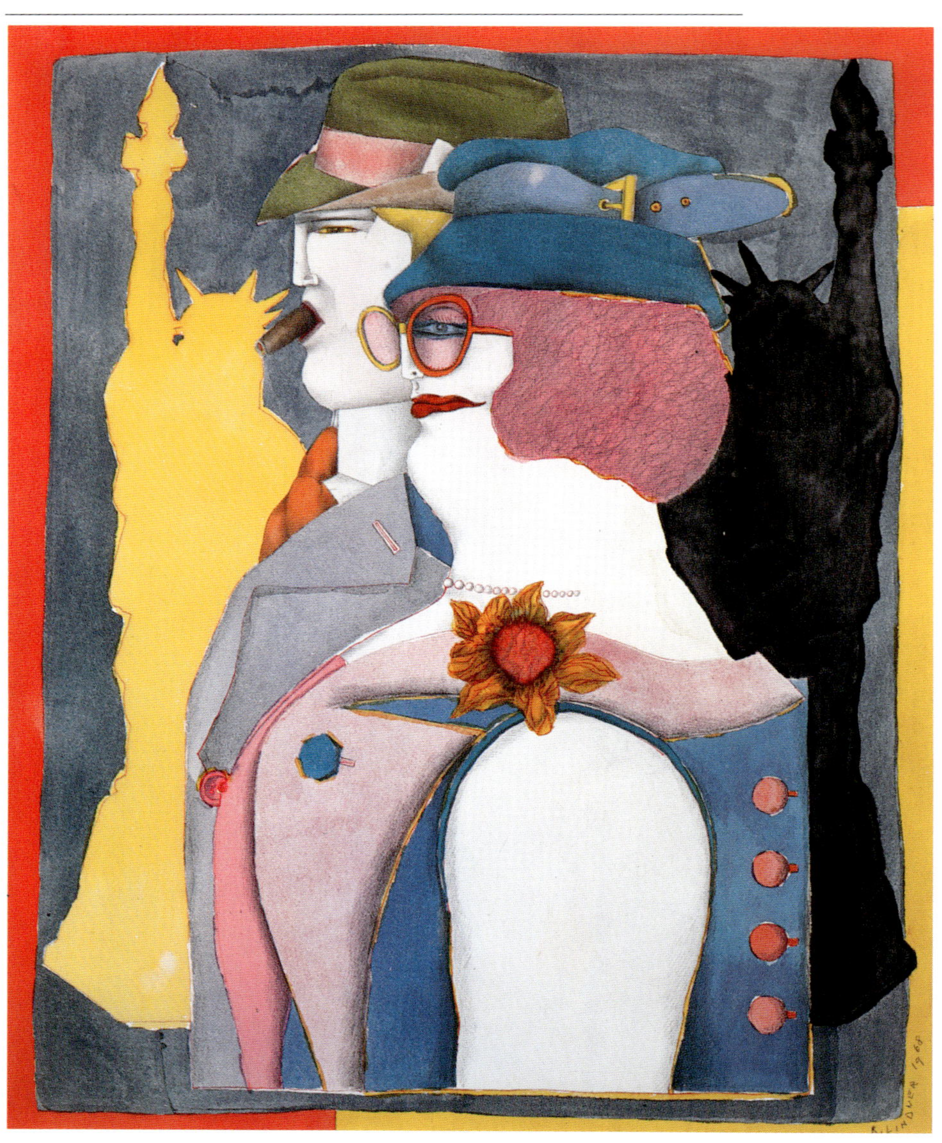

Nineteenth and Twentieth-Century American Painting

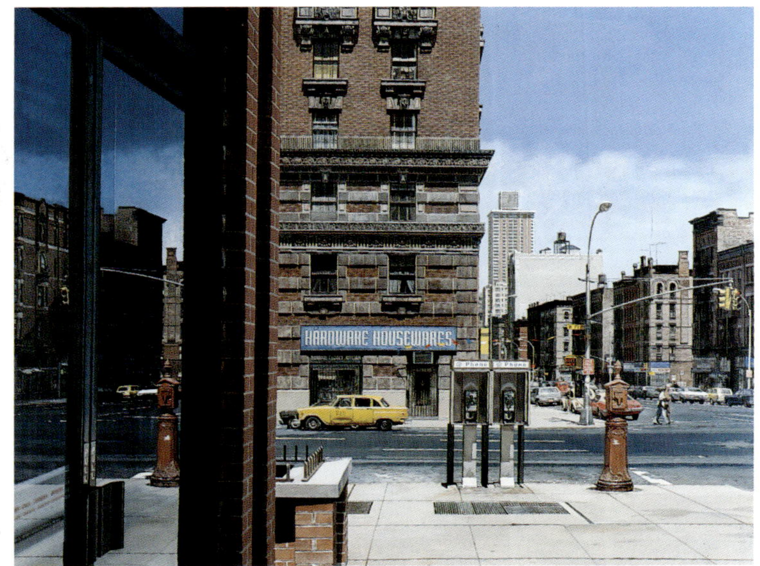

nates in a mute alliance of the past (specifically his youth in Weimar Germany) and the present, and his later experience as a "tourist"—as he liked to call himself—in New York after the war. In choosing the human figure as his vehicle for symbolic expression, Lindner belongs to an important group of post-war artists—including such important figures as Balthus and Francis Bacon—who never allied themselves with any group or movement.

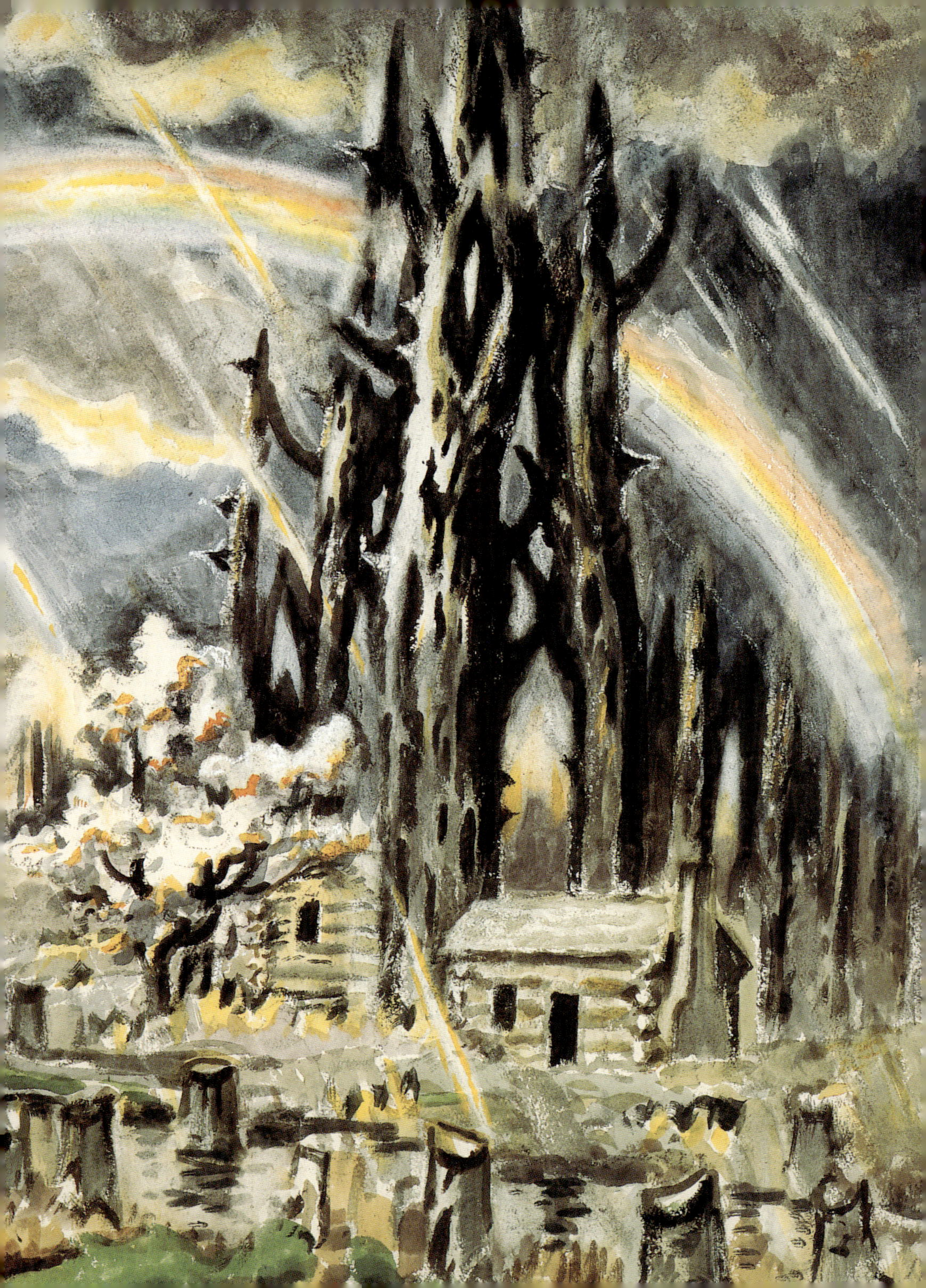

American Watercolour Painting[9]

[9] Certain works may not be on display as a result of their delicate nature.

The contribution of American artists to the history of watercolour painting has often been undervalued.

Although the English established the idiom and dominated the tradition for centuries, America produced a quantity and variety of works of unequalled mastery during the nineteenth century.

Watercolour is a particularly complex technique that can put even the best prepared artist to the test. This technique mixes water-soluble pigments with glue or fixative and superimposes layers of colour, from the darkest to the lightest. Their transparency makes retouching or correcting impossible. This factor, together with the rapid drying, makes watercolour a technique that demands speedy execution as well as confidence and the ability to improvise. These qualities only come with experience.

The rise of the watercolour coincides with the growth of American painting in general and was practised by the same artists. It is interesting to note that all these artists were interested in working in watercolour as a primary means of expression that rivalled oil painting. The fact that many American artists worked in this technique shows the influence that England still enjoyed in the United States. In any event, the technique that the Americans inherited from the English was already mature and had special qualities that American artists were able to use in a unique manner. As we will see when we observe the works of the greatest American watercolourists such as Homer, Hopper, Marin, Burchfield and Wyeth, there were as many approaches to watercolour in America as there were artists.

Among these, the most praised and admired is certainly *Winslow Homer* (1836-1910). Since the period in which they were executed,

Charles Burchfield
Dream of a Storm at Dawn, circa 1963-66, detail

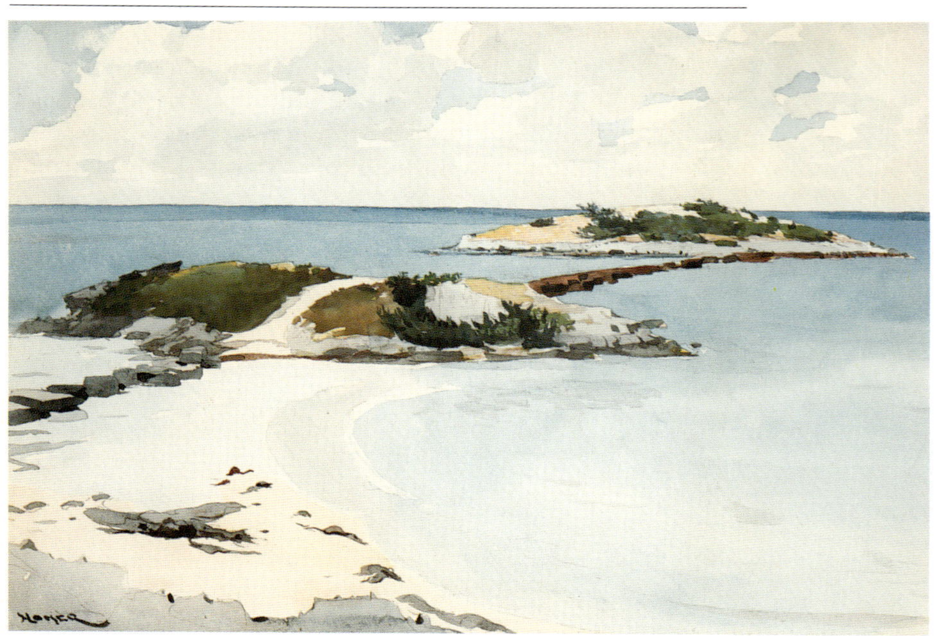

the works of Homer have been considered one of the finest expressions of American art. Carried out between 1873 and 1905, his works have lost none of their luminosity, immediacy of expression or economy of material. Unlike his oil paintings, to which he dedicated most of his life and which he worked on over long periods of time in his studio, his watercolours were created for the most part during his holidays in New England, the Adirondacks, Quebec, the Caribbean and Florida. The easy handling of watercolour and the speed with which it dries made it an ideal medium for a travelling artist like Homer and encouraged an intimate vision of nature that otherwise would not have found expression in his art.

Winslow Homer firmly believed that it was the painter's responsibility to portray the variety of the world while remaining faithful to himself. Remaining himself meant remaining American and thus aware of, but not a slave to, European artistic theories. Initially, Homer's watercolours were pleasant exercises rather than tradition-breaking statements. During his second trip to Europe in 1881, particularly during the two years he spent in the Northumberland fishing village of Cullercoats, Homer's work underwent a metamorphosis and his watercolours began to express the daring and force that were the distinguishing characteristics of his mature work in this

Winslow Homer
Gallow's Island, Bermuda, circa 1899-1901

American Watercolour Painting

medium. Homer rented a cottage at Cullercoats and observed the life of the village and the sea, recording what he saw in numerous charcoal, pastel, and watercolour sketches. While many of his paintings portray the men of Cullercoats, a still greater part depicts the women around these men, their wives, sisters and daughters. Upon his return to America, Homer found that the life of the big city was no longer useful for his work and in 1883 he moved to Prout's Neck in Maine. Here, in an oceanfront studio on the steep, rocky shore, the artist spent the rest of his life gradually moving towards a more direct aesthetic confrontation with nature; a confrontation that no longer depended on heroic fishermens' wives to act as mediators of the melodrama. Like many inhabitants of New England, Homer loved passing the winter in the English islands of the Caribbean, whose tropical landscapes seem deceptively easy to portray. Homer succeeded in doing so with great skill and facility as *Gallow's Island, Bermuda* (circa 1899-1901) demonstrates. It is a brilliant sketch of blue water and yellow sand, in which both the romantic side of his work and vision of nature appear. The watercolour *Early Morning in the Adirondacks* (1892) offers a rare example of a canoe appearing suddenly out of the mist and is witness to the artist's great interest in the lives of the hunters and fisherman he met during his trips to Quebec and the Adirondacks.

Homer's contemporaries John Singer Sargent and James McNeill Whistler were also great watercolourists, but none of their works are on display.

At the beginning of the twentieth century, *John Marin* (1870-1953) invented a completely new vocabulary, which allowed him to achieve a pre-eminent position among the pioneers who had begun Americanising the revolutionary art of Europe. Marin had spent much time abroad, particularly in Paris. When he returned to the United States—where he immediately entered Stieglitz' 291 Gallery—he turned to watercolour, modified European models and adapted them to the demands of his personal interpretation of New York's dynamism. Between 1910 and 1930, he produced a series of drawings and watercolours that manipulated the suggestive geometric forms of the skyscrapers that had just begun transforming Manhattan's skyline into semi-abstract compositions of great vitality. As we have seen, the modernity of the subjects became typical of much of avant-garde American art produced during the first three decades of the century. While European artists' inspiration to portray modern subjects came from their sensation of being surrounded by a mori-

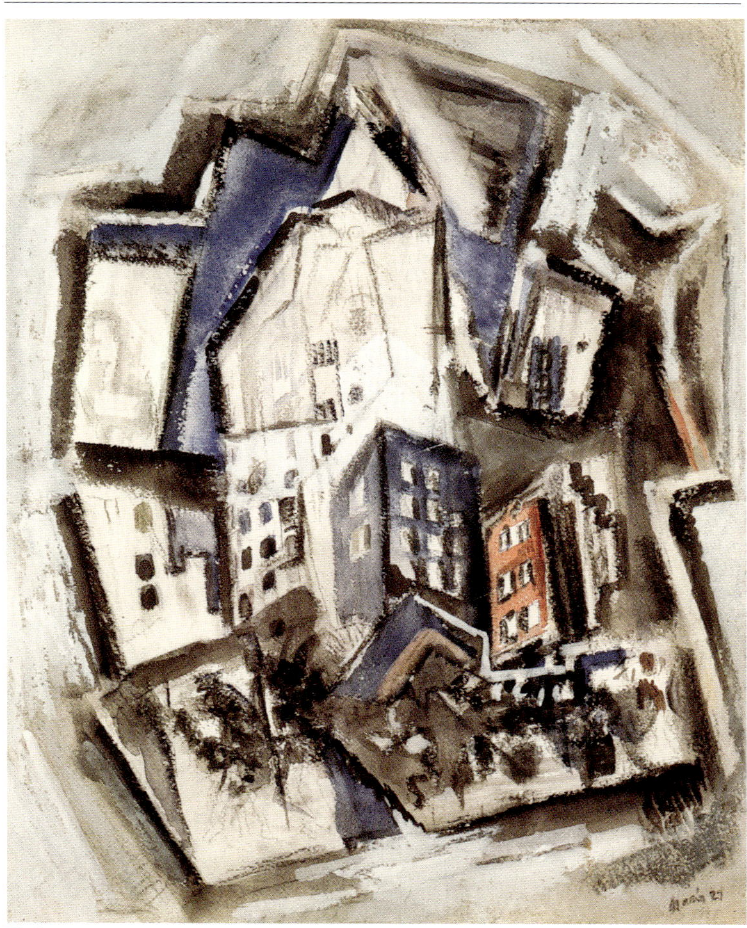

bund world, American artists saw new marvels springing up around them and felt that they could be faithful to the principles of modernism merely by narrating the architectural and mechanical marvels that surrounded them in their changing world. None of the conventional beauty of technique is visible in Marin's first watercolours. Their distinctive feature is a rigid calligraphic statement, in which the chromatic effects are achieved by placing the colours next to each other in a post-Impressionistic manner, rather than superimposing transparent layers of colour. Naturally, recording architectural and mechanical wonders did not mean, at least in Marin's case, that artists were satisfied with conventional realism. Marin used expressionistic exaggerations and post-Cubist fragmentation to suggest the frenetic

American Watercolour Painting

quality of urban life. He sought life in city buildings, which appears clearly in the watercolours he did between 1912 and 1913 as well as those from between 1920 and 1922. Marin himself said of his first watercolours: "Shall we consider the life of a great city as confined simply to the people and animals on its streets and in its buildings? Are the buildings themselves dead? We have been told somewhere that a work of art is a thing alive. You cannot create a work of art unless the things you behold respond to something within you. Therefore if these buildings move me, they too must have a life. Thus the whole city is alive; and the more they move me the more I feel them to be alive". In his watercolours of the 1920s (see *New York*

Charles Demuth
Church in Provincetown, No. 2, 1919

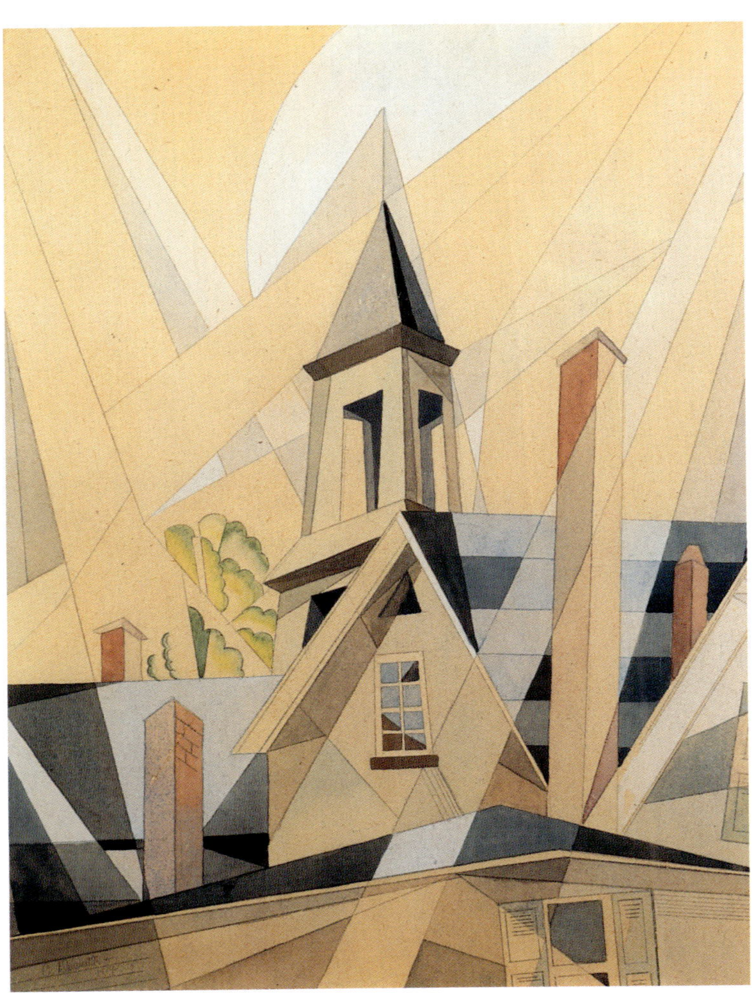

Series of 1927 in the gallery), Marin departs from a point at ground level and then makes decisive use of conventional perspective to create a sense of dimension. Strong black lines begin defining the composition and the city seems as if it is about to explode; the buildings seem fragmented as if they were based on the Cubist and Futurist practice. The city was not the only subject that inspired Marin. If his attempts to infuse skyscrapers and bridges with life suggest a kind of industrial pantheism, it is not surprising that when he treated nature he was indeed inspired by the true pantheism of Thoreau and Emerson. Nor is it surprising that he was attracted to landscape painting, especially seascapes (see *Eastport, Maine,* 1933). Landscape forced Marin to confront problems very different from those of the growing city; with landscape he had to deal with a theme that painters, and watercolour painters in particular, had struggled with for generations. The subject itself offered no inherent guarantee of contemporary relevance. If he wanted to be a modernist when nature was the subject, he had to impress it with his own stamp of originality. He felt that there was a mysterious vital force that pervaded the entire natural world and it was his theory that the colours and forms of nature could never be accurately captured on paper. He preferred to believe that his hand would be guided by the same force that made the wind blow and made the tides rise and fall.

The other great watercolour painter during the first three decades of the twentieth century was *Charles Demuth* (1883-1935), who owed his fame as a still-life painter to the studies of flowers, fruit and vegetables that he began doing around 1915. The collection includes two of these, one of tulips and the other of zinnias. These are extraordinarily direct and are delightful examples of what can be achieved by the simplest of means if the artist's hand and eye are confident enough. These still-lives recall the work of Cézanne, especially their use of blank white areas. Cézanne's influence on Demuth, who could have seen his works in the Paris apartment of Gertrude Stein, is important to keep in mind, especially when viewing the watercolours of angular landscapes and city views inspired by Cubism. These semi-abstract compositions may be compared to landscapes painted by other artists such as *Lyonel Feininger* (1871-1956) (see *Street Behind the Church. Treptow an der Rega,* 1931). In these works by Demuth, space is not fragmented and reordered as it is in Cubism. Instead a geometric grid, based on the artist's memory of Cubist works and manmade structures visible in the landscape, serves as a structure on which tiny, naturalistic details may be suspended in shal-

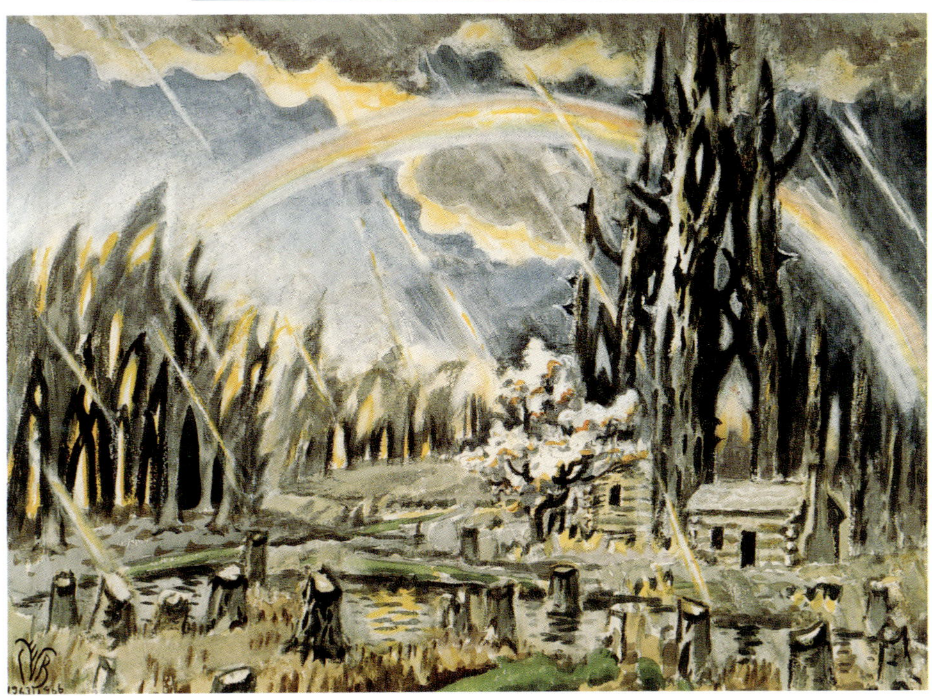

low space. An example of the application of this grid to an American town can be seen in the work *Church at Provincetown, No. 2* of 1919.

No other American artist derived so much inspiration from his childhood environment as *Charles Burchfield* (1893-1967). Nor did any other American artist, including Marin, use watercolour in the same way and with such intensity. Like many artists during the first decades of the twentieth century, Burchfield was fascinated by the idea of parallels between art and music and by the idea that painting could become a universal language with forms and colours playing the same role as musical notes whose function was not strictly descriptive. He even did a few drawings in which he sought to give visible substance to works by Richard Wagner. After studying at the Cleveland Institute of Art, Burchfield received a scholarship to the National Academy of Design in New York, although by 1917 he had already returned to Salem, where he had grown up. Here he realised an enormous number of sketches in the open air. He also painted in his small bedroom and developed his own Expressionistic idiom. In his watercolours, Burchfield used calculated distortions of form to amplify his emotional state, proof of his indisputable awareness of the works of

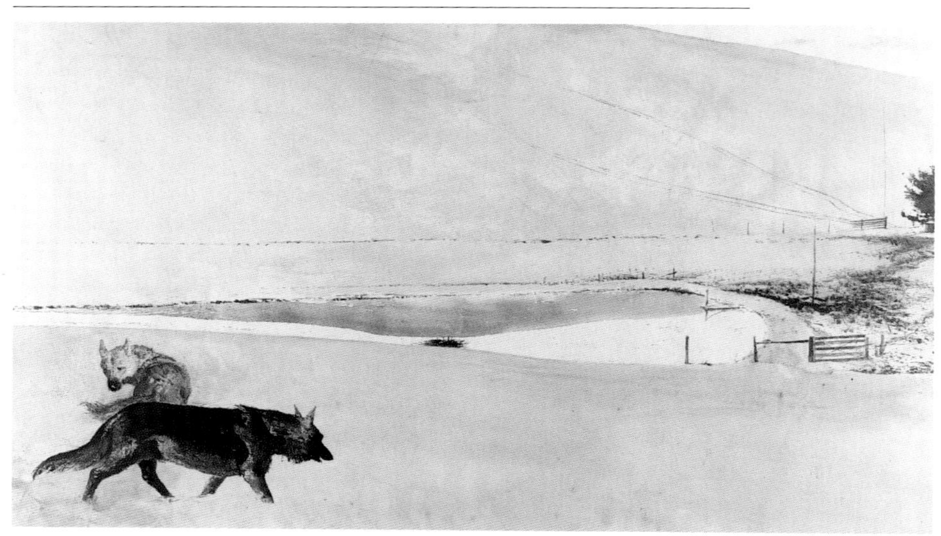

Andrew Wyeth
Malamute, 1976

van Gogh and Munch and probably those of the Expressionists. Nevertheless, he expressed himself in a completely personal manner that was rooted in his observation of the landscape of the Ohio that he knew so well. This period of intense activity ended when Burchfield joined the army towards the end of First World War. The collection owns a watercolour from this period entitled *Haunted Evening* (1919). Like Marin Burchfield seems to have sensed a godlike force inhabiting all of nature and it is the unifying power of this force that he celebrated in his art. In the 1920s, Burchfield began to be interested in a more naturalistic treatment of urban and rural subjects, which would remain central to his work throughout the following two decades. In the 1940s, he returned to his younger works for inspiration, as if he desired to find primary sustenance in nature. If seen from a strictly iconographic point of view, the works from this period no longer feature architectonic forms that impersonate natural forms, as they did in his earlier works, but natural forms that imitate architecture. We can see this transformation in works such as *Dream of a Storm at Dawn* (1963-66), where the trees have metamorphosed and seem to have become the arches of a gothic building.

Edward Hopper (1882-1967) was almost Burchfield's contemporary. Unlike Burchfield, who worked almost exclusively in watercolour, Hopper usually worked in oil; in fact, his watercolours are more easily understood when seen in relation to his oil paintings. Hopper's watercolours, to which he applied himself with greater inter-

American Watercolour Painting

est after his fortieth year, are characterised by the honesty and accuracy of his vision. In fact, his watercolours illustrate the idea of solitude in the city and the technique itself contributes to the impression that the artist places the viewer in front of an urban desert. Unlike Homer, Hopper did not use watercolour as if it were an almost sublime act of pleasure, but used it as an intellectual instrument that helped define his relationship with the physical world. Two works by Hopper, *My Roof* (1928) and *Rocky Cove* (1929), are on display in the collection.

In more recent years, the artist who has done the most to perpetuate the realist watercolour tradition is *Andrew Wyeth* (b. 1917). His interest in the common people of Pennsylvania and Maine put him in a position that is far removed from most of his contemporaries. It is not only his subjects that render his art unique, but also the manner and the intensity with which he analyses them. Wyeth's world seems untouched by the frenzy of urban America (see *Malamute* of 1976); his world is one where people and places only change over time. Wyeth's "dry brush" technique is particularly suitable for capturing every wrinkle in a man's face or every brushstroke on a barn wall. Even if Wyeth's world changed more slowly than the rest of America, the artist was not unaware of these changes. He did not depict a lost Arcadia, but rather depicted what he saw with a basic honesty that is characteristic of his time.

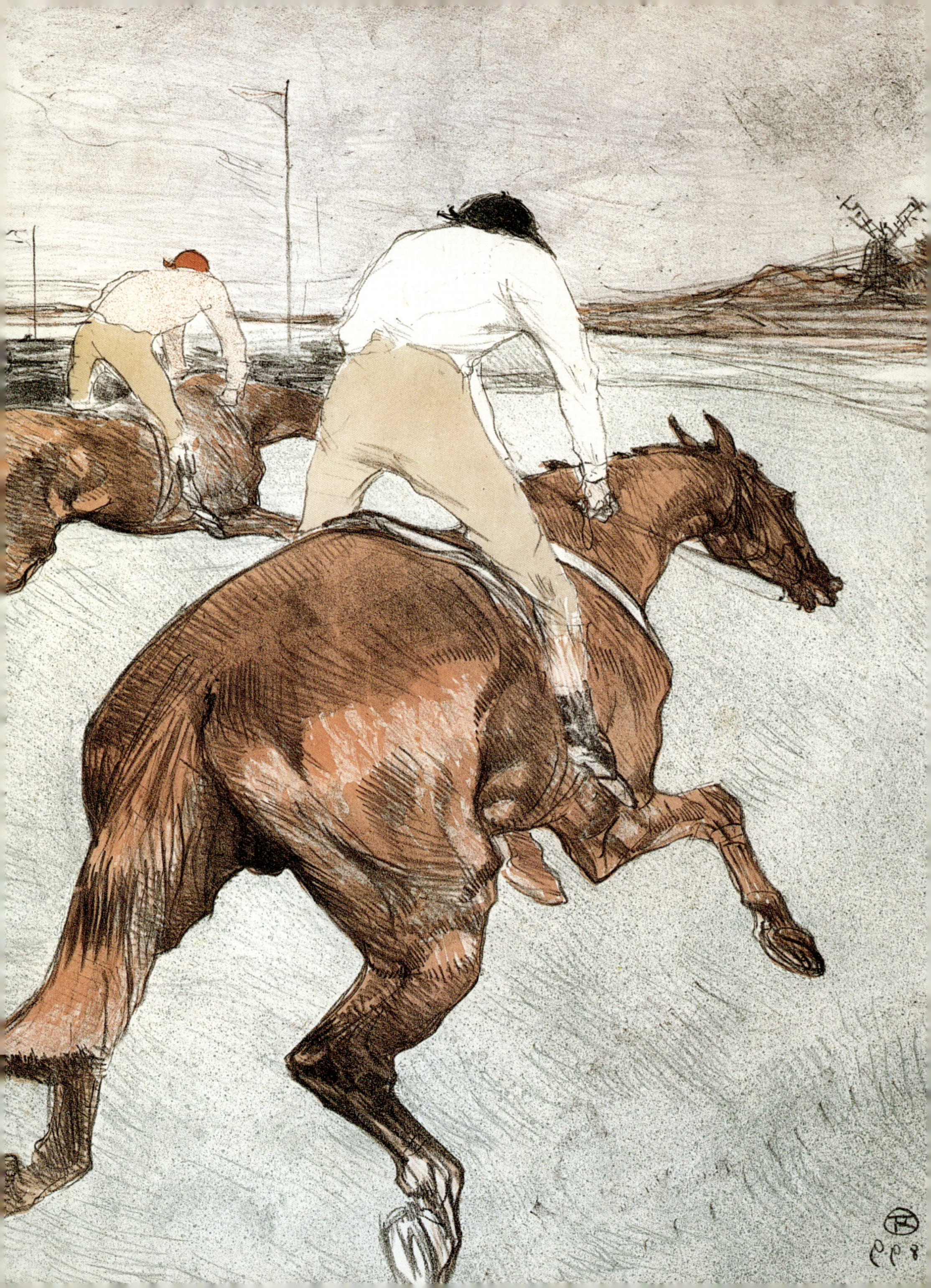

Henri de Toulouse-Lautrec

Few artists have captured the imagination of the public as effectively as Henri de Toulouse-Lautrec. His biography adheres perfectly to our ideas of artistic suffering and social rebellion: born to an aristocratic family, as an adolescent he was the victim of a series of accidents that left him lame. He found solace in alcohol and the company of the Paris *demi-monde*. Throughout his life he moved between two different and opposed worlds, testing the limits of both, but never effectively cancelling the social frontiers of his class and type. In a few words, Lautrec was the quintessence of a bohemian, moving between the centre and the fringes of bourgeois life. The centre of Lautrec's world was the nocturnal life of Paris during the 1880s and 1890s, with its cabarets, bars and brothels.

Toulouse-Lautrec was twenty-seven when, in 1891, he was commissioned to do his first advertising poster: *Moulin Rouge: La Goulue* was such a success that similar commissions quickly multiplied. Toulouse-Lautrec was so gratified by this success that he fervently dedicated the remaining ten years of his life to this new form of expression and produced more than three-hundred fifty prints, the majority of which were lithographs. During those same years, many artists who were dissatisfied with traditional means of expression shared a common interest in the graphic arts. Lautrec was particularly attracted by Japanese prints, from which he learned that sacrificing shading and other details in favour of bold simplifications gave new strength and persuasive power to his works.

The splendid group of Toulouse-Lautrec lithographs in the Thyssen-Bornemisza collection makes it easy to follow the development of his graphic style from the type of simplicity similar to the posters (such as

At the Moulin Rouge: La Goulue and her Sister and *Englishman at the Moulin Rouge*) through to the late masterpiece *The Jockey*. The singers, dancers and actors that Lautrec portrayed in his last ten years achieved immortality through his works: for example Yvette Guilbert, one of the most famous entertainers of the time or Mlle. Cha-U-Kau. The famous series of prints entitled *Elles* dates from 1896, when it was published by Gustave Pellet (see *The Sitting Female Clown*). In 1897, the same publisher brought out a strictly limited edition of the equally well-known coloured lithographs that confirmed Lautrec as one of the greatest print artists of the nineteenth and twentieth centuries: *La Grande Loge, Elsa, la Viennoie* and *The Female Clown at the Moulin Rouge* are among these.

After his death in 1901, even Parisian night life was destined to change. The Moulin Rouge was closed by its owner and the dance hall became a conventional music hall. The amusements that had been launched for the Parisian public became shows for tourists; many other dance halls later became cinemas. In the mid nineteen-twenties, the large panels that Lautrec had painted to advertise La Goulue's shows became part of the French national collections and the by-now poor and forgotten entertainer was reduced to selling matches on street corners.

The night life of Paris was not the only theme that captured Toulouse-Lautrec's interest. Beginning in 1898, he turned his attention to horses, female riders and the world that gravitated around racetracks, which became another of his principle subjects. To understand the importance of this theme, we must also understand the important role that horses had played in Lautrec's education. His father, who considered himself an admirable sportsman, took his son to the stables every day in the hope that riding could strengthen and improve his son's physique (as an adolescent he broke both legs twice). However, as the years passed, the shortness of the artist's legs became an increasingly insurmountable handicap. All of his biographers discuss what a deep loss Lautrec felt that his incapacity was for him. For example, his friend Thadée Natanson recalled that he had "a great passion for horses and he never got over not being able to ride. To create the illusion that he was riding, while the yoke of his open carriage supported him, he leaned dangerously out, and pressed up against his mounted friend. This gave him the illusion of being attached to the horse" (Whitfield, 1990). It is just this perilous closeness between the artist and horse that transforms *The Jockey* into one of the most vigorous and penetrating of Lautrec's lithographs.

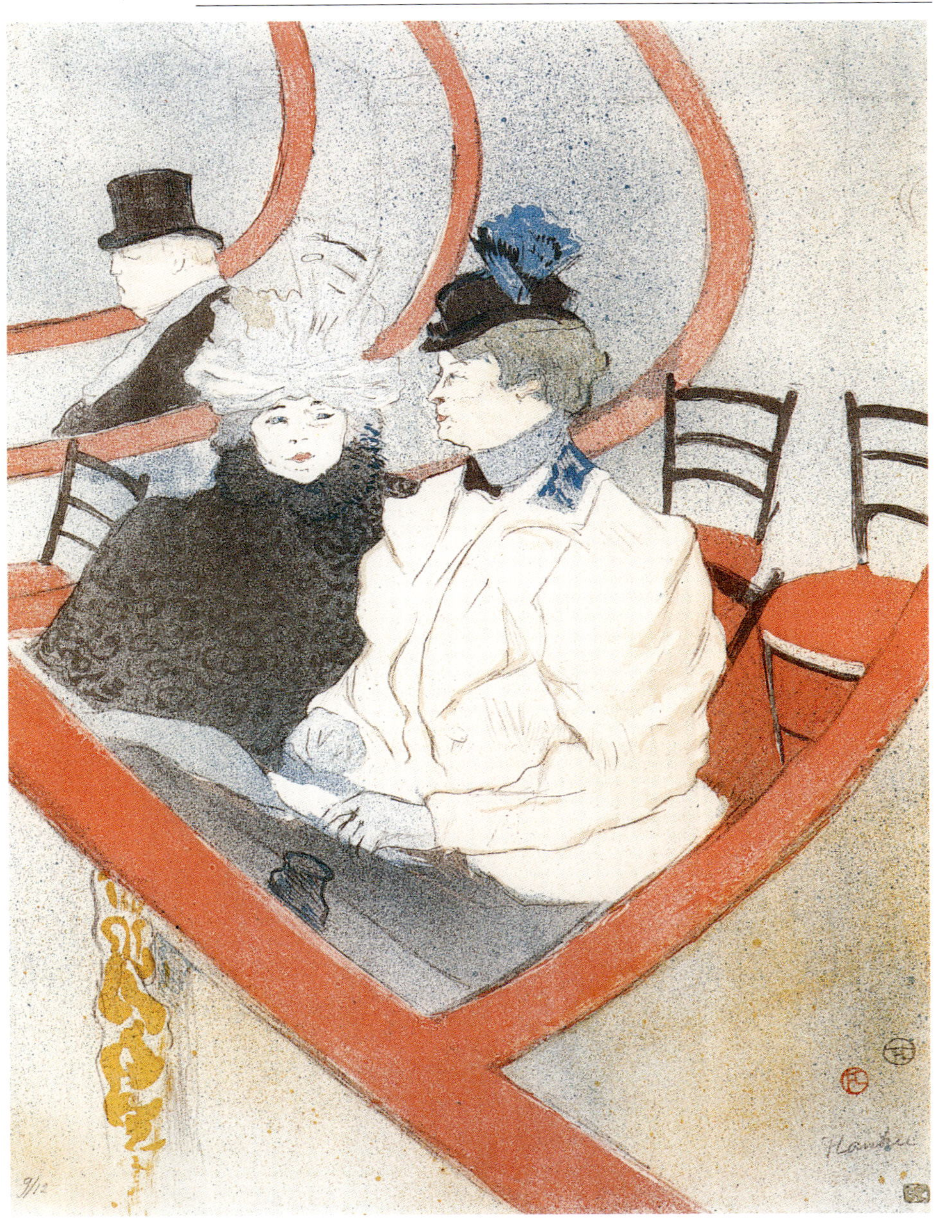

Henri de Toulouse-Lautrec

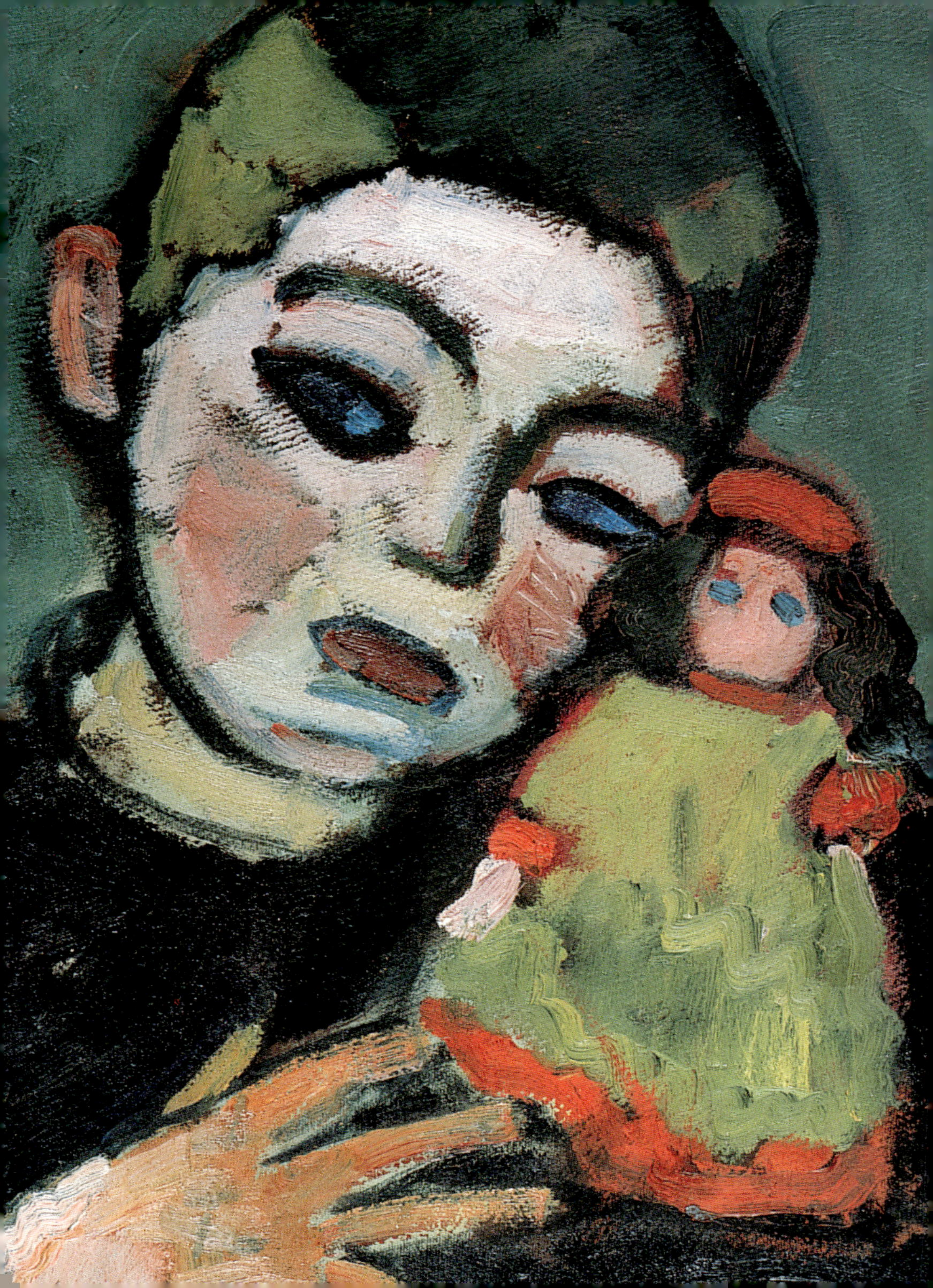

German Expressionism: A Personal Choice

Hans Heinrich Thyssen's collection of modern art began with his acquisition of a watercolour by Emil Nolde. In an article that appeared in *Apollo* in 1983, he describes the genesis of his recent passion: "It was the early 1960s that I purchased my first work by a German Expressionist artist. It was a watercolour by Emil Nolde of circa 1931-35 showing a young couple. I had instantly been struck by its bold colour range and by the very particular atmosphere that emanated from it. I acquired it at an auction held at the Stuttgarter Kunstkabinett. Two friends of mine, Stavros Niarchos and David Rockefeller, had introduced me to the owner and auctioneer of that firm, Mr. Roman Norbert Ketterer. This man was to become a good friend who guided my first steps in the nearly unknown territory that was for me then twentieth-century art. During my youth my father had always brain-washed me that twentieth-century art was of little interest. For a long time I believed him and for fifteen years after his death I bought solely Old Master paintings. Gradually I began to think that every artistic effort that was being done in the first half of this century at a time when major achievements had been made in most areas could not be totally devoid of interest. I soon became a regular client at the auctions held twice yearly in Stuttgart. This not just for the red roses that were distributed by Ketterer to collectors who had successfully emerged from fierce bidding battles. After the Nolde watercolour came works by Erich Heckel, Pechstein and Ludwig Kirchner who is perhaps my favourite Expressionist German painter. To start with I knew little about German Expressionist paintings and I began to study and read about the subject. The fact that these artists had been oppressed by the National Socialistic régime and that their art had been officially branded as being degenerate, was for me an added incentive for collecting them. For years I had been unsuccessfully trying to find on the market a major work by Franz Marc. My persistence eventually was to be rewarded when I could acquire *The Dream* of 1912. Marc was a fellow member of Wassily Kandinsky in the 'Blaue Reiter' Group. Like that I began to become very interested in Kandinsky which then led to me becoming actively involved in acquiring works by members of the Russian avant-garde and more generally works by pioneers of abstract art".

Expressionism, as Peter Vergo observed in the catalogue raisonné of the Thyssen-Bornemisza collection (London 1992), is the most difficult "movement" to define in the history of the art of this century. What one can say is that Expressionism represents, in a general sense, reactions to both Impressionism and to Naturalism as well as a widespread rejection of the simple recording of natural appearances and the transcription of actions or events. This term may also be applied to all art whose source is the emotional or spiritual experience of reality expressed through powerful colour and incisive drawing. Even if Expressionism was not a coherent set of convictions or principles, it did however present a common vision of the world. This vision was profoundly influenced by nineteenth-century German idealistic philosophy, particularly Nietzsche and Schopenhauer: disdain for science and mere observation, faith in the power of the artist to create images of the world as it should be; the notion that reality is concealed behind the superficial appearance of things, which means that normal processes of observation and deduction are incapable of revealing it although it may be grasped in the aesthetic sphere. These artists affirmed their presence in visible, technical signs such as strong brush-strokes or outlines.

In the field of the figurative arts, Expressionism found its basic principles in the work of painters of anguished subjects or painters who had reacted against Impressionism, such as Edvard Munch, James Ensor, Vincent van Gogh or Paul Gauguin. There were representatives of the movement in Belgium and Holland (Constant Permeke, Gustave de Smet and Jan Toorop) as well as in France (Chaïm Soutine, Marc Chagall and Frantisek Kupka). The most fertile terrain for Expressionism was Germany.

The full, formal realisation of Expressionist taste came with the formation of the group Die Brücke (The Bridge) in Dresden in 1905 by Ernst Ludwig Kirchner, Fritz Bleyl, Karl Schmidt-Rottluff and Erich Heckel. Whether inspired by their direct experience of post-Impressionist works, contact with romantic and gothic art, African sculpture and folk art, these artists established original and diverse styles of their own. Their manifesto, which Kirchner carved in wood, declared: "With faith in progress, in a new generation of creators and viewers of art, we mobilise all young people. As youth who hold the future in our hands, we want to conquer the freedom of action and life denied by the deeply rooted forces of the old. We want with us whoever is moved to create with sincerity and directness". *Karl Schmidt-Rotluff* (1884-1976) seems to have been the inventor of the name Die Brücke. There are numerous interpretations of its meaning. For example, Kirchner declared that in the minds of the group members it represented a bridge to the future. However, there is little doubt that the name was an implicit allusion to Nietzsche's *Thus Spoke Zarathustra*, in which the author often refers to a "bridge towards superman" (Vergo 1989).

Lead by a desire to recapture primitive simplicity, these artists found their themes in the "natural" condition of man (anecdotes about their scandalous lifestyles proliferated). For their models they chose streetwalkers and cabaret artists who they portrayed nude out-of-doors and with whom they shared their crowded studios. The theme of the nude in a landscape is one of the most frequent in their works. The collection owns *Nude by a Woodland Pool* by *Otto Müller* (1874-1930) as a means of confronting themes related to political and urban reality. Graphic arts, particularly woodcut prints, became one of the group's favourite media.

The reaction of the public and the official world to Die Brücke's exhibitions was hostile, or non-existent. The German bourgeoisie was as much disturbed by the violence the Expressionists did to beauty as by the way they deformed nature. While it is taken for granted that the caricaturist may reveal man's ugliness—it is his role to do so—an artist who is to be considered "serious" is not permitted to brutalise instead of idealise. The Expressionists were so deeply sensitive to human suffering, violence, misery and passion that insisting on the harmony and beauty of art seemed hardly honest. Avoiding anything that suggested grace or careful craftsmanship, scandalising the bourgeoisie and shaking its complacence became points of honour for the Expressionists. The lack of consensus did not disturb them as they felt that their allegiance to Nietzsche and their role as artists put them above normal people, who had less will and creative power or did not share their superior vision of the world in which they saw things not as they are but "more completely and with greater simplicity and

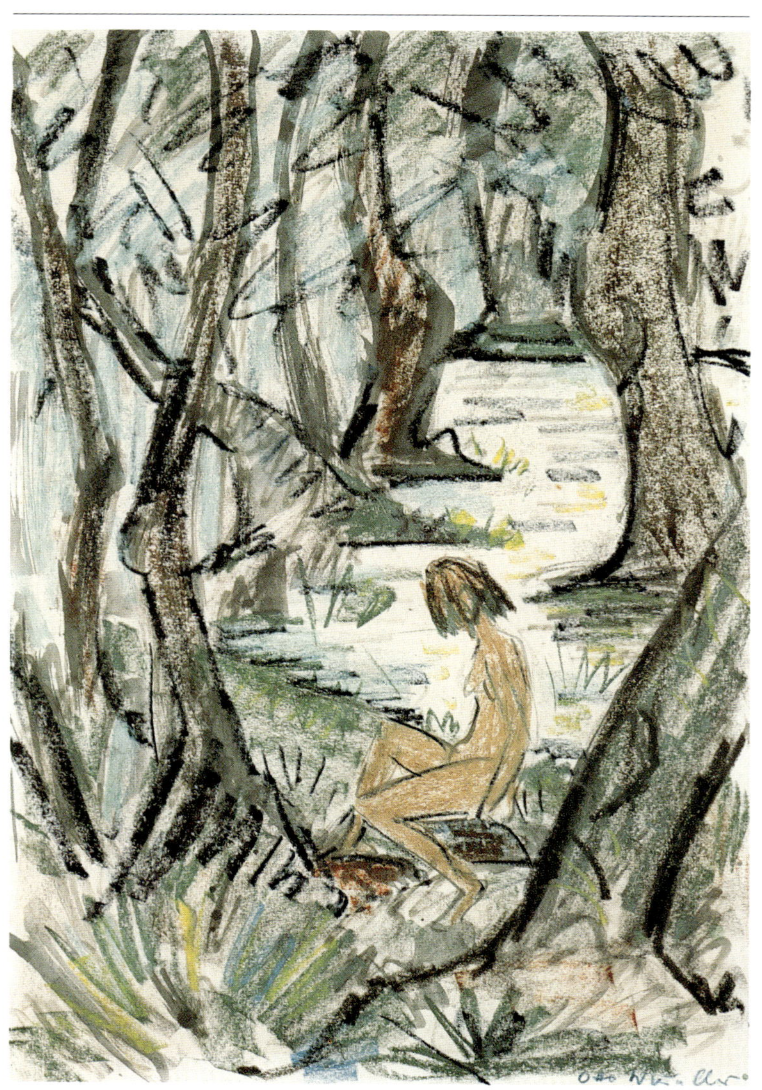

Otto Müller
Nude by a
Woodland Pool,
circa 1920-22

German Expressionism: A Personal Choice

force". In 1911, Die Brücke moved to Berlin, where it disbanded two years later, leaving its individual members to continue working independently.

Similar ideas inspired other groups including the Neue Künstlervereinigung (New Artists Association) founded in Munich in 1909 and Der Blaue Reiter (the Blue Rider) movement established in 1912. The emphasis of the latter was on expressive abstraction and was promoted by artists such as Wassily Kandinsky, Paul Klee, Franz Marc and August Macke and, more marginally, *Alexej von Jawlensky* (1867-1941). There was close and fruitful contact between the groups and the Die Brücke artists often participated in the Blaue Reiter group's exhibitions. Kandinsky and Marc also published works in the Blaue Reiter's famous almanac, which was a sort of annual compendium of contemporary art. Only artists, including musicians, rather than critics or art historians were asked to contribute. Both groups responded to similar experiences: van Gogh, modern French painting, primitive tribal art, the philosophy of Schopenhauer and Nietzsche. Their differences showed up—strongly—in the subjects they chose to depict and to a certain extent in their differing beliefs about art. The Blaue Reiter and Kandinsky's abstract theories about the artist's messianic role were foreign to the artists of Die Brücke, who were interested in tangible and visible reality, the human figure, nature and the landscape (see Schmidt-Rottluff's *The Village of Dangast* of 1909), the sky and forest and the world around them. The Blaue Reiter group dispersed with the outbreak of First World War, in which Marc and Macke lost their lives.

The collection has the only watercolour that *Franz Marc* (1880-1916) did while in the army, *Cup with a Fox and a Deer* (1915); it is also his last work. The figures decorating this strange cup attest to the artist's interest in animals, which he considered symbols of spirituality and the vital force. Marc's great friend *August Macke* (1887-1914) painted the small watercolour in the collection entitled *Flowers* of circa 1913, which may have been a design for fabric.

In 1924, three of the members of the avant-garde active in Munich during the pre-war period, Klee, Kandinsky and Jawlensky joined with the American Lyonel Feininger to form the group the Blue Four.

A few painters who have been loosely classified as Expressionists, in reality did not belong to any of the groups described above. Nonetheless, it is conventional to call them Expressionists (Vergo 1989) as a result of certain characteristics of their work: distortion of

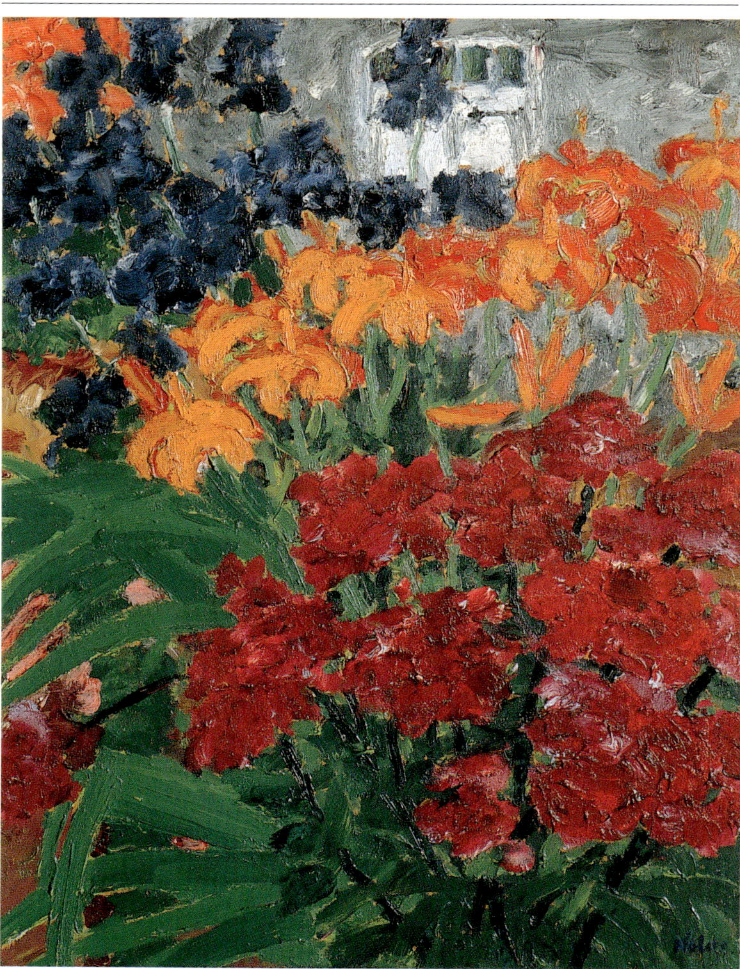

Emil Nolde
Flower Garden,
1917

anatomy or perspective, extremely intense colour, little interest in faithfully recording nature, a desire to penetrate the surface of things, to expose their essence (we can see this in Jawlensky's painting in the collection, *Child with a Doll,* of 1910).

A special place among these artists is held by *Egon Schiele* (1890-1918), who lived in tragic solitude in Vienna. *Boy in a Sailor Suit* of 1915, is an example of both his extraordinary ability as a draftsman, and of the erotic undercurrent of his art, which shocked and scandalised the bourgeoisie of the time. The boy portrayed is Paul Erdmann, Schiele's wife's nephew.

Meidner, Feininger and Beckmann, who were active about the

German Expressionism: A Personal Choice

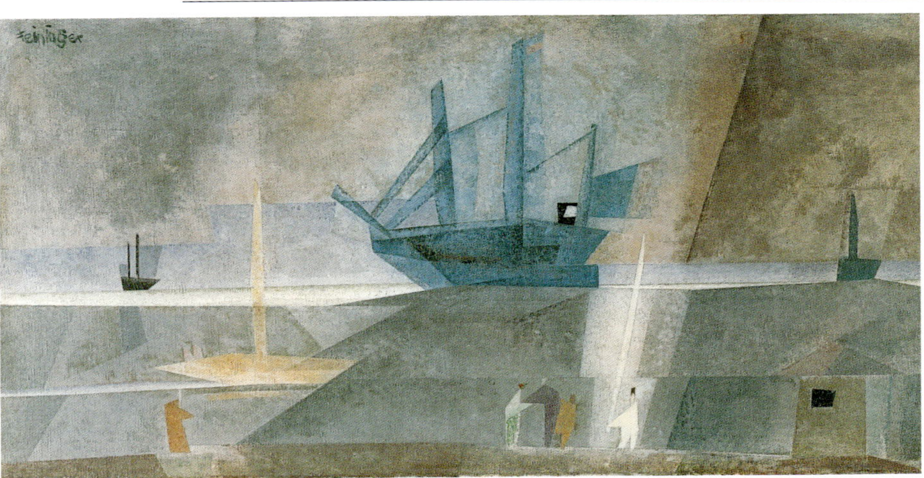

Lyonel Feininger
*Magic River
(Dream Across
the River)*, 1937

same time, were also part of this group of "independent Expressionists". Even though he is often referred to as German artist, *Lyonel Feininger* (1871-1956) was actually American and his work was influential in making the Blue Four known in America, where Feininger returned in 1938 when it became clear that he had no future in Nazi Germany. Feininger's *Magic River (Dream Across the River)* of 1937, his last year in Germany, is charged with the artist's hopes for the future. It is an imaginary scene, probably based on Feininger's recollection of actual places. The dark colour accentuates the composition's sadness. The influence of the French Cubists and Feininger's origins as an illustrator can also be seen in *La Belle* (1906), a preliminary study made for the painting that is in the Thyssen-Bornemisza collection in Madrid.

When the Nazis came to power in 1933, all contemporary art was banished and the most important exponents of the modern movement were forced into exile or prohibited from working. *Ernst Barlach* (1870-1938), the only Expressionist sculptor of importance (see his bronze *The Terrorized* of 1912), as well as the great *Emil Nolde* (1867-1956) were both victims of this treatment. Nolde may be considered the prototypical German Expressionist. He was more independent than others and lived in self-imposed solitude. When he was eighty, he observed, "How happy I am to be virtually alone as an artist among other artists, with the crowds of other artists somewhere else". His development as a painter was not isolated however; he worked in parallel and often quite closely with other artists. He appeared in the first exhibitions of Die Brücke and shared the joys and failures of the

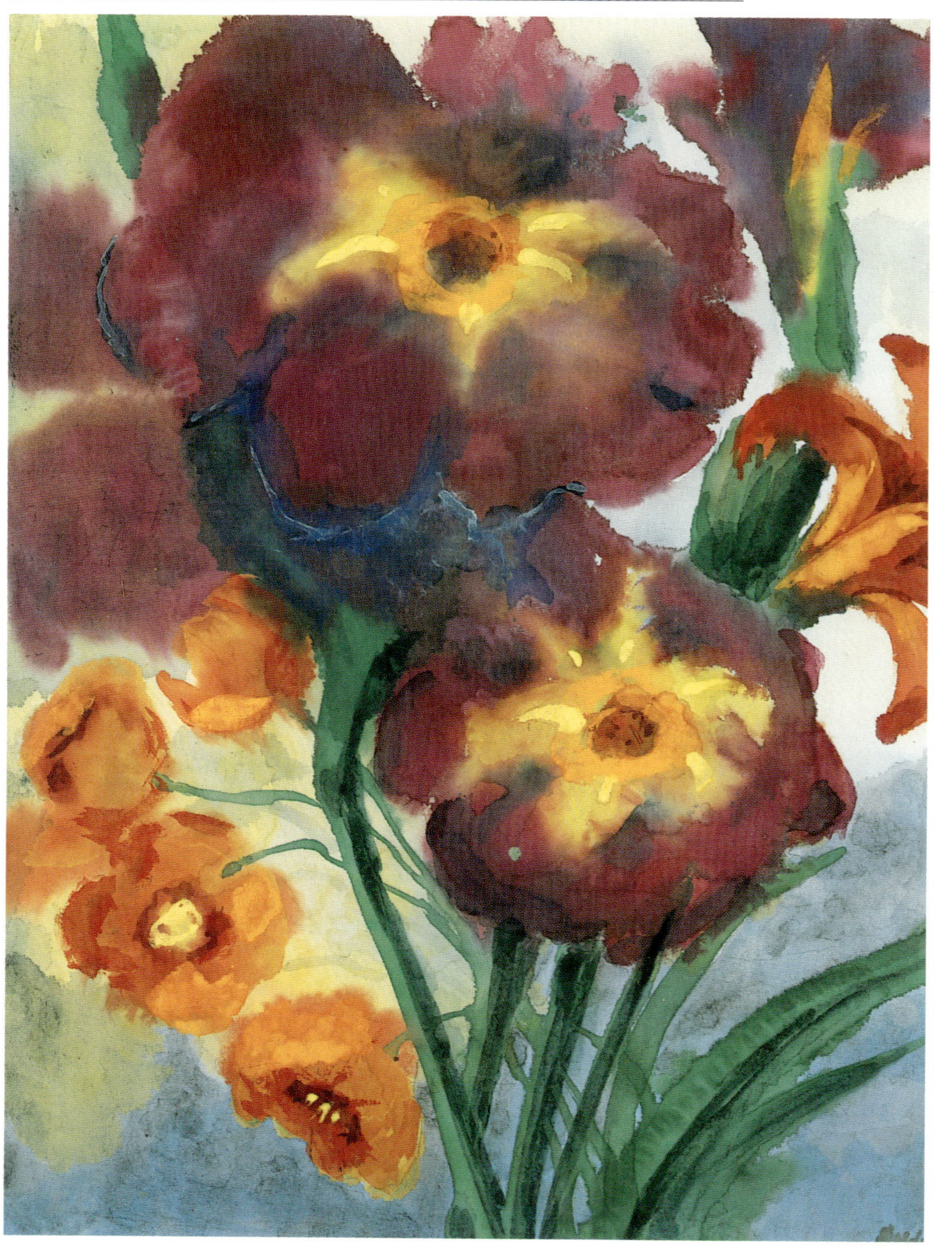

German Expressionism: A Personal Choice

Emil Nolde
*Iris, Tiger-Lilies
and Poppies,*
circa 1930-35

Ernst Barlach
The Terrorized,
1912

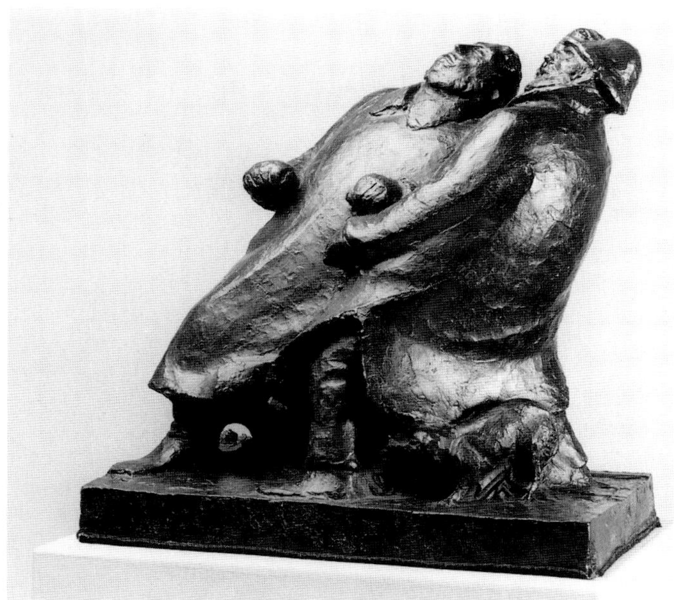

group's artists. His "storms of colour" gained him acceptance in the group of painters, but by 1907 Nolde had already left Dresden in search of those landscapes that could satisfy his desire—common to other German Expressionists—to fuse the individual with the cosmos, the internal and the external worlds. On the coast of the North Sea, Nolde found a place that seemed to satisfy his desire (see *Landscape with Farms* of 1946, the year that his wife Ada died and one of his first post-war works). While painting gardens and flowers Nolde discovered the evocative power of colour (see the *Flower Garden* of 1917). His relationship with flowers was unusual, almost physical, as he wrote in his autobiography: "It seems as if they love my hands", or "Yellow stands for joy as well as pain", and "colours are the notes that I use to create sounds and chords". He also described the life cycle of flowers that, "sprout, flower, shine, are resplendent, give cheer, languish, wilt and end up as rubbish". The gardens of his last house at Seebüll, on the border between Denmark and Germany, were the splendour of the place and it was here that Nolde realised some of his most beautiful works. *Summer Flowers (Red and White Poppies against a Blue Sky)* and *Iris, Tiger-Lilies and Poppies,* both in the collection, were probably painted at Seebüll in the 1930s.

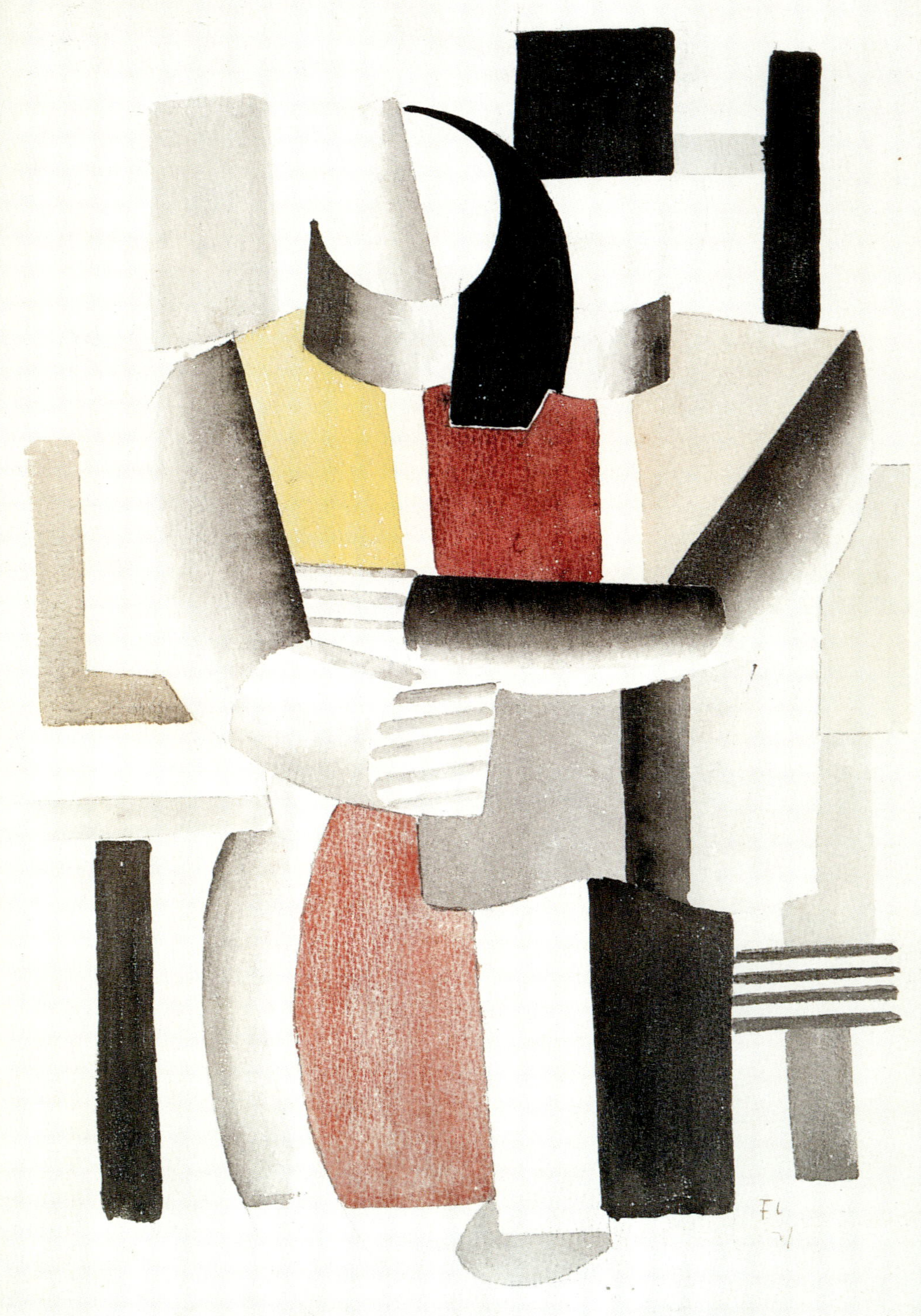

The European Avant-Garde
Michele Sottile

The period between the end of the last century and First World War saw a series of changes in the political, economic, social, philosophical and scientific fields that also influenced the artistic panorama. The so-called "historic avant-garde" was intertwined, sometimes unconsciously or rather without the direct participation of the artists, with the new philosophical and scientific theories that were being worked out at the same time. "Avant-garde" was the term used to define the numerous artistic and cultural groups whose work and research put them in opposition to the academic artistic tradition. The very choice of the name "avant-garde", which was taken directly from the political and military vocabulary, reveals the desire of its adherents to break with and make an attack on traditional artistic positions. The avant-garde movements saw themselves as a renewing force and believed that the only possible means of renewing art was to make a leap out of the past and into the future. Many of these groups, but not all, felt a need to give form to their ideas, aspirations and poetic meaning by presenting them in manifestos. Some of these manifestos were disregarded, while others, such as that of the Futurists, anticipated the course of the movement itself. These were years of great cultural ferment and energy.

Among the works of the so called "Avant-garde" present in the picture-gallery of the Villa Favorita, the part of the lion is played by the Russian artists. The more or less sixty paintings collected by Baron Thyssen-Bornemisza between 1973 and 1991 constitute first of all an important contribute to our understanding of the artistic experiments pursued in Russia during the first decades of the twentieth century: until recently, very little was in fact known about these paintings due to the particular political situation in Russia at the time. The inaccessibility of the Russian archives and works in fact caused the few paintings that arrived in the West to do so illegally and without any indication regarding their provenance. These paintings also represent the last chapter of the history of collecting Russian art in the West. The adventure involving the collection of Russian art had been pursued, during the second half of the century, by other collectors such as George Costakis, Peter Ludzig, Nina and Nikita Lobonov-Rotovsky, Thomas Whitney; this venture, however, could not be repeated nowadays. The reasons for this are not exclusively financial, but are rather to be attributed to the fact that the Soviet and Western sources have been practically exhausted. Thanks to the enthusiasm of Baron Thyssen-Bornemisza, the names of many artists have been saved from oblivion and have assumed a legitimate position in the history of Russian culture. The following pages are dedicated to these Russian artists' experiments which are narrated in parallel with those of contemporary Western artists.

In 1907 the Salon d'Automne featured a major retrospective exhibition of the works of Paul Cézanne. He was the first who spoke of "treating nature in terms of cylinders, spheres and cones" and his influence was decisive for the kind of painting that, because it emphasised geometric volumes, came to be called Cubist. The Cubist painters' greatest desire was to show reality not as it appeared, but rather as it was perceived by the mind. While Cézanne was the inspiration behind the Cubist movement, its actual founders were Pablo Picasso, Georges Braque, André Derain; later Fernand Léger, Juan Gris and Robert Delaunay followed in their wake. With his *Portrait of Gertrude Stein* and *Les Demoiselles d'Avignon*, Picasso ignited a revolution in the artistic world and brought Cubism to life. His bond with Braque was fundamental for the whole of twentieth-century art. Robert Delaunay followed his own inclination with respect to the rest of the Cubists and Apollinaire considered him a "heretic". Colour and light held a prominent position in his search for non-objective painting. In 1912-13 he painted a series of disks based on the colour wheel. During the same years, Apollinaire announced the birth of a new movement: Orfism, whose name was inspired by the poetry of Apollinaire himself, who tried to gather together all the artists that he felt belonged to his classification insofar as they spoke a "luminous language" expressed in painting.

The Thyssen collection contains some interesting works of these movements including: *Fernand Léger's* (1881-1955) *Man and Woman*

Gino Severini
*Still Life with a
Bottle of Marsala,*
1917

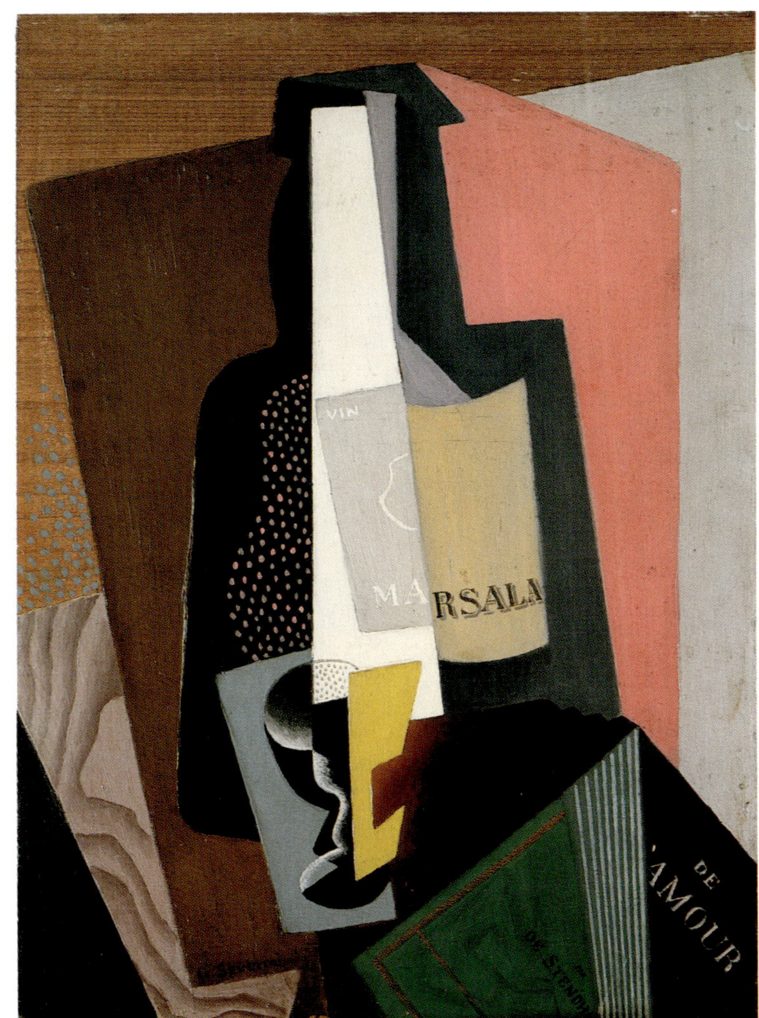

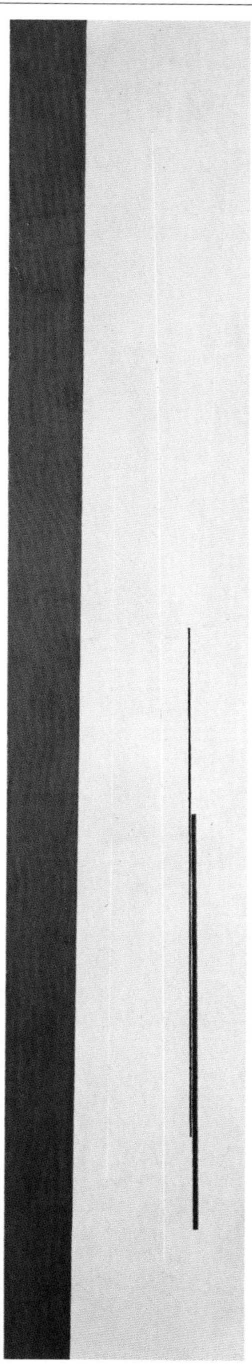

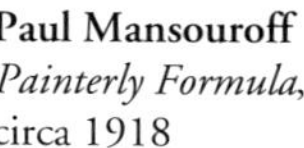

Paul Mansouroff
Painterly Formula,
circa 1918

The European Avant-Garde

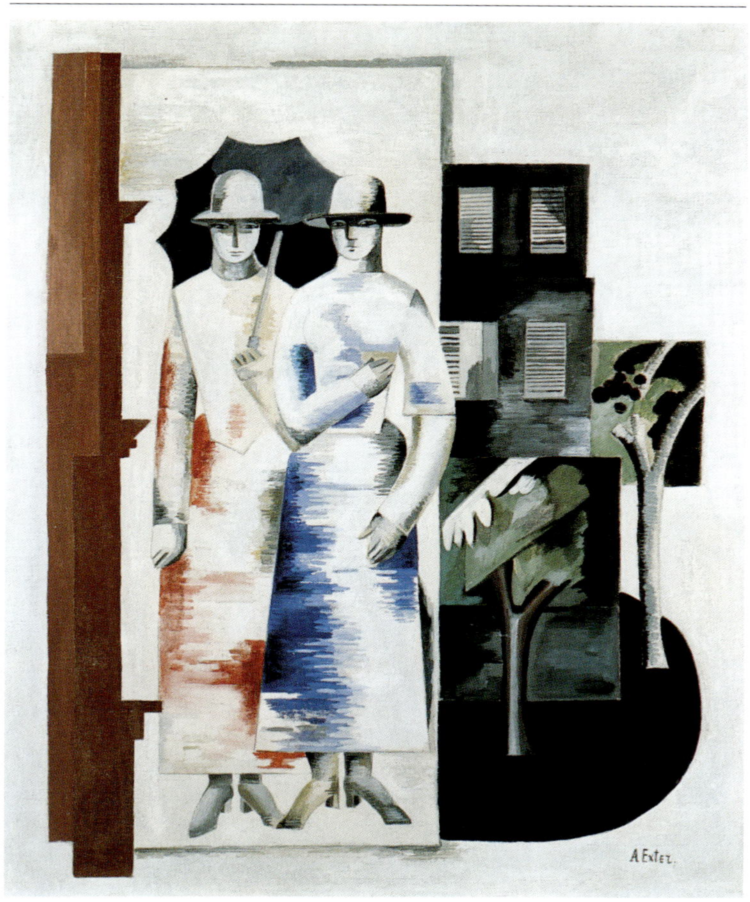

Alexandra Exter
Two Women in a Garden, 1927

(watercolour) of 1921, a work from his "mechanical period" which began right after his experience in First World War; and *André Masson's* (1896-1987) *The Statue* of 1925. This painting is part of a series of still-lifes and compositions inspired by Cubism, including *Gino Severini's* (1883-1966) *Still Life with a Bottle of Marsala* of 1917.

A few Russian artists such as *David Nestorovich Kakabadzé* (1889-1952) (*Untitled,* 1920) and *Vladimir Lebedev* (1891-1967) (*Cubism: A Portrait,* 1920) also produced highly personal interpretations of Cubism that still remained within the style's conventions; and *Olga Vladimirovna Rozanova* (1886-1918) did *Urban Landscape* in 1912 and it is typical of the fusion of Cubist and Futurist elements that took place in Russia and was called Cubo-Futurism. The painter *Marie Vassilieff* (1884-1957) also fit into this group and her work

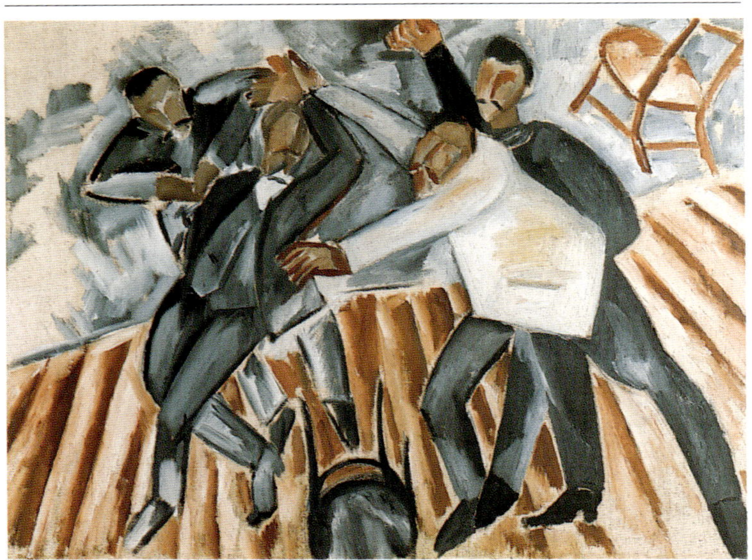

Woman with a Fan (1910) is a classic example of this artist's Cubist work and her beginnings studying with Matisse in Paris.

The manifesto of Rayonism appeared in Russia in 1913 and was signed by *Mikhail Larionov* (1881-1964) as well as thirteen other artists including his companion and collaborator Natalia Goncharova. The manifesto of Rayonism declared that "the Rayonist style of painting that we promote is concerned with the spatial forms that occur when the rays reflected by various objects or forms chosen by the artist intersect". Rayonism was directly inspired by Cubism, Futurism, and Orfism and sought to blend the experiences of the European avant-garde with Russian artistic culture. In the collection we can see Larionov's *The Brawl* (1911) from his neo-primitivist period.

In addition to Rayonism, the Russian avant-garde expressed itself in Suprematism, which was the creation of *Kazimir Malevich* (1878-1935). In the Suprematist manifesto, which was also signed by the poet Vladimir Mayakovsky, Malevich stated that Suprematism was to mean "the supremacy of pure sensitivity in the figurative arts". Malevich followed the artistic work of Larionov and Goncharova with interest, but soon went off in other directions. Although the Villa Favorita collection holds only one of Malevich's works, *Untitled* (circa 1919), it is possible to do a brief tour of the style through the works of other exponents of Suprematism.

There are two works by the Russian painter *Ksenia Vladimirova*

The European Avant-Garde

**Ilia Grigorievich
Chashnik**
*Suprematist Relief
No. II*, circa 1926

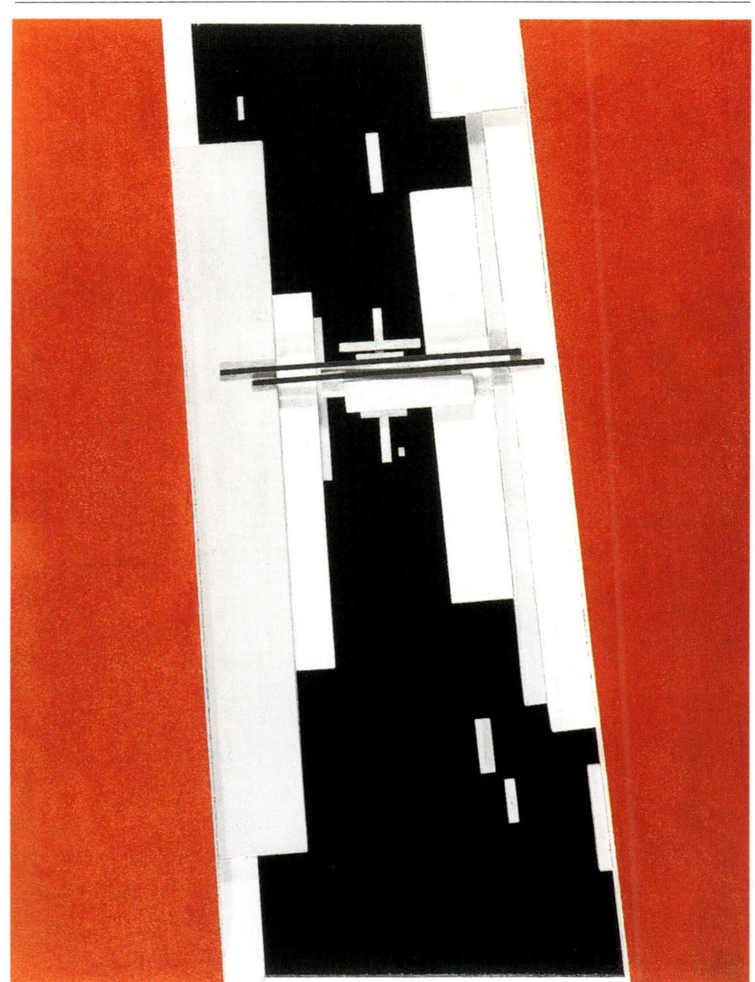

Ender (1894-1958), *Untitled* (1918), which is directly inspired by Malevich's Suprematist compositions, and *Composition* (1918), which reflects the Futurist work of Balla and Boccioni.

The Russian painter *Varvara Fedorovna Stepanova* (1894-1958) is represented in the collection by *Two People at a Table* (1921), in which the human figure has been reduced to flat shapes, mere coloured shapes. Another representative figure of the Russian avant-garde was *Nadezhda Udaltsova* (1886-1961), who has two works on display: *Composition* (1916) and *Untitled* (1917), both of which show how the painter had assimilated Malevich's theory of Suprematism.

Alexandra Exter (1882-1949) was another female protagonist of the Russian avant-garde who experimented with the Cubist, Futurist, Suprematist and Constructivist styles. We may see her *Two Women in a Garden* (1927), which is directly inspired by the painting of Léger. In fact, Exter also taught at Léger's Académie d'Art Contemporain in Paris. Continuing our look at the Suprematists in the collection, we come across two works by *Ilia Grigorievich Chashnik* (1902-1929). After graduating from the Institute of Applied Arts at Vitebsk, of which Malevich was the head, he collaborated with him and worked for the Lomonosov porcelain factory. His rich, but brief, artistic career—he died at age twenty-seven—was important for the history of the Russian avant-garde. Two of his works are in the collection: a small pencil drawing and watercolour entitled *Composition* (circa 1924), whose geometric elements laid out in a fan shape are typical of his style, and *Suprematist Relief No. II* (circa 1926), which is part of a series of squares, rectangles, lines and overlapping circles organised in a Suprematist syntax. Reliefs like this seem as if they were imaginary architectural models and are similar to the projects of Vladimir Tatlin, who in the same years had produced architectural utopias such as the *Monument to the Third International* of 1919-20. This innovative and revolutionary work was halfway between architecture and sculpture and was part of the Constructivist movement.

Constructivism was founded in Russia in 1915 by Vladimir Tatlin and Naum Gabo and was based on the same figurative assumptions as contemporary Western movements such as Cubism, Dadaism and Futurism. It rejected bourgeois art and sought a new artistic vocabulary in the fields of technology and industrial mechanics. Among the exponents of Constructivism in the collection are *Paul Mansouroff* (1896-1984), who had studied at the Stieglitz Institute of Painting in St. Petersburg. During his service in the czarist air force he worked as a mechanical draftsman, where he refined his notable graphic skills.

                                              The European Avant-Garde

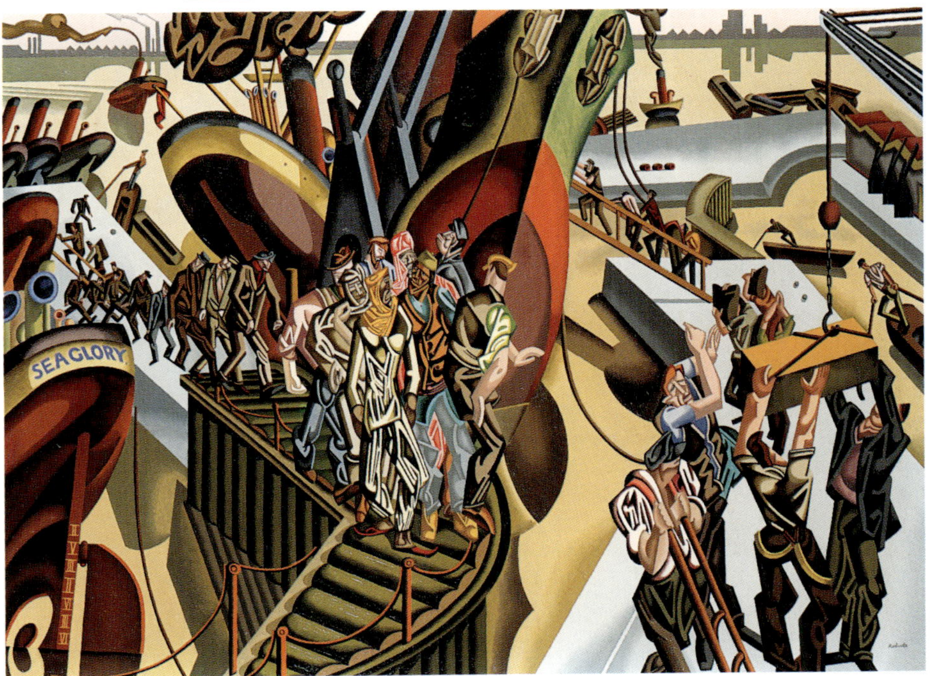

William Roberts
Dock Gates, 1920

Precision and fine strokes subsequently became the defining characteristics of his work. The collection displays his *Painterly Formula* (circa 1918) and *Untitled* (circa 1923-24).

Futurism was the most subversive of the avant-garde movements. It was born when Filippo Tommaso Marinetti published his *Futurist Manifesto* in *Le Figaro* February 20, 1909. This manifesto had a very strong impact. Its incendiary effect sparked a proliferation of young enthusiasts of the new Futurist vocabulary. In 1910 the *Manifesto of Futurist Painters* was signed by the artists Umberto Boccioni, Carlo Carrà, Giacomo Balla, Luigi Russolo and Gino Severini. It was followed in 1914 by the *Manifesto of Futurist Architecture* signed by Antonio Sant'Elia. The movement sought total rupture with the past and longed for a complete and radical renewal that would accept no compromises with tradition and the "leavings" of past generations. The key words were: modernity, industrial civilisation, speed and progress. Within the movement artists experimented with new vocabularies for all forms of expression: literature, painting, the graphic arts, photography, cinema, theatre and clothing. The movement owed its great success to the histrionic skills of many of its members who organized encounters with the public. These were the famous "Futurist

Evenings", where the public was forced to participate and become the protagonist of these "happenings". The collection features two works by *Gino Severini* (1882-1966), who was one of the signers of the *Futurist Manifesto*: the *Still Life with a Bottle of Marsala*, from the painter's Cubist period, and a work of 1950 entitled *Pas de Deux No. 1*, which is an example of the Cubist-abstract style typical of his late works.

The collection also has a work by *Félix Del Marle* (1889-1952), who published the *Futurist Manifesto against Montmartre* with Marinetti, entitled *Triptych: 1 The White Line, Prélude. 2 The White Line, Fugue. 3 The White Line, Finale*. This work is the result of the artist's search for non-objective painting that has strong metaphysical aspirations and close ties to music.

Futurism generated the English Vorticism, propounded by Wyndham Lewis. Lewis was a follower of Marinetti who brought a new aesthetic of speed, machines and industrial civilization to Britain. He was immediately supported by the poet Ezra Pound, who became the ideologue of the movement. Vorticism disbanded immediately after

The European Avant-Garde

the horrors of First World War. There are two Vorticist works in the collection by *William P. Roberts* (1895-1980), who met Lewis in 1914 and adhered to the Vorticist manifesto as well as being invited to participate in the first issue of the Vorticist review *Blast*. These are his *War Celebration* (1919) and *Dock Gates* (1920). The latter, which is a celebration of labour's productivity and industry, is one of the most significant works of the movement.

After seeing the English experience, we return to the continent to find one of the most interesting artistic groups of the avant-garde active at the time.

In Holland, abstraction assumed the form of yet another new movement, Neoplasticism whose official organ was the review *De Stijl*. The leaders of this movement were Piet Mondrian and Theo van Doesburg. Artists belonging to the Neoplasticism (New Form) movement sought to establish an equilibrium between the "universal and particular". The elements of their works were lines and colours whose abstract purity was intended to overcome the individualistic aspects of artistic creation. For them, art had to overcome reality, which they considered antithetical to the spirit. They searched almost obsessively for logical and impersonal structures of reality that would eliminate the natural aspect of things, which is what renders them tragic. Form was suppressed and visual possibilities were reduced to a single straight line, which is the synthesis of all other forms. Likewise they limited themselves to the primary colours that are the origin of all other hues: red, yellow and blue were rigidly inserted on white fields delimited by black lines. There are some examples of this movement in the Thyssen collection starting with *Composition No. 5M, Lozenge* (1926) by *César Domela* (1900-1992), where Mondrian's strong influence can clearly be seen. Domela also worked for several years in Switzerland before entering Mondrian's and Doesburg's circle in 1924. The painting *Black-Blue (Large Square)* of 1922 by *Karl Peter Röhl* (1890-1975) was illustrated in *De Stijl* and belongs to the important series of works that he did in the years when he was at the Bauhaus, Walter Gropius' art school where, for the first time, theory and practical applications were thoroughly integrated. *Johannes Itten* (1888-1967) whose *Kindly Light* (1963) is exhibited here, also worked at the Bauhaus. This painting develops the theme of light through its use of colour. The collection also contains a work by *Walter Dexel* (1890-1973): *Skyscraper* of 1923. He was part of the De Stijl group, even if Constructivist elements began to appear in his work during the later phases of his career. The painting *Skyscraper* belongs to a

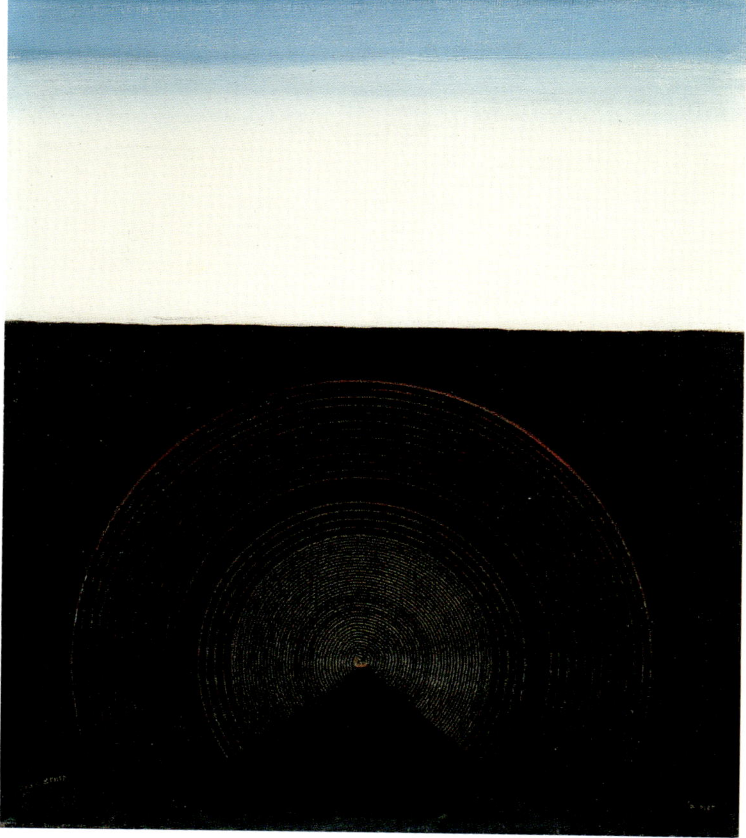

series of works dedicated to the city and its architectonic forms show an unmistakable Constructivist influence.

The Dada movement which originated in Zurich in 1916 may be considered a sort of "appendix" to the European avant-garde. Dadaism rejected all theories, any rules or stylistic coherence. In fact Dadaism was not a school but rather a negation of the academic teaching of art. Its very name, itself part of the "program", was born of "a whim of folly that came from nowhere". The figures behind this movement were the poet Tristan Tzara, who had a leading role, along with artists such as Marcel Duchamp, Francis Picabia, Man Ray, Hans Arp, Marcel Janco, Sophie Tauber and Hugo Ball. The Dada movement did not seek to "create" but rather to "fabricate" from existing objects and material. It rejected traditional artistic conven-

The European Avant-Garde

tions and experimented with materials that had never been used by artists before. It sought to go beyond the avant-garde and proclaimed its demise.

Eight years after it began, the movement spawned Surrealism which inherited its innovative momentum and iconoclastic and provocative spirit from the Dada movement. The Surrealists were interested in dreams, psychoanalysis, automatic writing and those zones of the unconscious that belong to "sur-reality" which can only be reached via insanity, hallucination or the imagination. The only unifying feature of the Surrealists' work was their predilection for powerful and visionary images; in fact they shared virtually no stylistic traits. According to them, Freudian techniques were necessary for bringing images to the surface from the depths of the unconscious. The major figures of the Surrealist movement were Max Ernst, Joan Miró, André Masson, Salvador Dalí, Yves Tanguy, Paul Delvaux and René Magritte. In the collection, Surrealism is represented by three works by *Max Ernst* (1891-1976), who was one of the founders of both the Dada and Surrealist movements: *The Sea* (1924), which is an enigmatic painting dominated by a circle, a figure that the painter was to use in later works such as *The Red Sun* (1957), also in the collection; *Loplop Présente la Belle Saison* (1930) is part of an extensive series dedicated to the bird Loplop, a metaphorical figure that represented the artist himself. *Francis Picabia* (1879-1953) was a fundamental figure in the Dada group and his *Le Broyeur* (1921-22) is part of a series of watercolours treating mechanical themes. The collection also owns *The Keyhole* (1928) by *Man Ray* (1890-1976), an American who spent most of his life in Paris where, with Picabia and Duchamp, he was a key figure in bringing the Dada movement to New York. This painting was done at the height of his Surrealist period and represents the fascination exercised by a keyhole that presumably opens onto a forbidden scene.

The greatest inspiration behind Surrealism was certainly *Giorgio de Chirico* (1888-1978). His imaginary places suspended in space and time served as a point of departure for many of the Surrealist painters. The two works by de Chirico in the collection warrant a space of their own: *Portrait of Young Woman with an Apple* (1921) and *The Solitary Archaeologist* (1966), which is one of the many paintings by the Italian artist where the figure of the automaton or the mannequin appears. In this painting, figments from the figure's memory seem to have visibly accumulated on his body which is composed of architectural remains; the head is enigmatically faceless.

The first Baron Thyssen loved Old Master art. In little more than twenty years the second Baron has collected almost one-thousand works ranging from the French Impressionism to the European avant-garde to American hyper-realism, of which we have tried to give a brief description in the preceding pages. This collection is an impressive enterprise that is witness to an interest in the various types of modern artistic expression as well as in the ability to span different periods and create trends. Just as it would no longer be possible to assemble a collection of Old Masters as extensive as the one put together in the 1920s by the father of the current Baron Thyssen for the simple fact that such works are no longer available on the market, likewise it would be impossible to unite paintings by the artists of the Russian avant-garde. Baron Hans Heinrich Thyssen-Bornemisza collected his works by these artists when very few were interested in them; he did the same with nineteenth-century American paintings.

The gallery of Villa Favorita aspires to be a witness to the interests of the two men whose lives and personal passions have written a chapter of the history of collecting that cannot be repeated.

Selected Bibliography

Apollo Magazine
CXVIII, no. 257: issue totally devoted to the Thyssen-Bornemisza collection, July 1983 (in English).

Bowlt, John E., Misler, Nicoletta
Twentieth-Century Russian and East European Painting. The Thyssen-Bornemisza Collection, London 1993.

Cottini, Paolo
Il giardino di Villa Favorita, Varese 1996.

Finch, Christopher
American Watercolors, New York 1986.

Gerdts, William W.
Impressionismo americano (exhibition catalogue, Villa Favorita, Lugano), Lugano 1990.

Green, Christopher
The European Avant-Gardes. The Thyssen-Bornemisza Collection, London 1994.

Howat, J.K.
The Hudson River School and Its Painters, Harmondsworth 1978.

Levin, Gail
Twentieth-Century American Painting. The Thyssen-Bornemisza Collection, London 1987.

Lucian Freud. Paintings
(exhibition catalogue, Washington, Paris, London, Berlin), London 1987.

Maestri americani della Collezione Thyssen-Bornemisza
(exhibition catalogue, Villa Malpensata, Lugano), Milan 1984.

Novak, Barbara
Nature and Culture, New York-Toronto 1980.

Novak, Barbara
Nineteenth-Century American Painting. The Thyssen-Bornemisza Collection, London 1986.

Penny, Nicholas
The Materials of Sculpture, New Haven-London 1993.

Radcliffe A., Baker M., Maek-Gerard M.
Renaissance and Later Sculpture. The Thyssen-Bornemisza Collection, London 1992.

Rose, Barbara
*American Painting. The Twentieth
Century*, Geneva 1980.

Storm Nagy, Elisabeth
*Europa e America. Dipinti e acquerelli
dell'Ottocento e del Novecento dalla
Collezione Thyssen-Bornemisza*, Milan
1993.

Vergo, Peter
*Espressionismo. Capolavori della
Collezione Thyssen-Bornemisza*
(exhibition catalogue, Villa Favorita,
Lugano), Milan 1989.

Vergo, Peter
*Twentieth-Century German Painting.
The Thyssen-Bornemisza Collection*,
London 1992.

Whitfield, Sarah
*Impressionismo e postimpressionismo.
Collezione Thyssen-Bornemisza*, Milan
1990.

Williamson, Paul
*Medieval Sculpture and Works of Art.
The Thyssen-Bornemisza Collection*,
London 1987.

List of Works

Paintings

Avery, Milton Clark (1885-1965)
Homework, 1946
Oil on canvas, 91.4 × 61 cm
1978.58

Benton, Thomas Hart (1889-1975)
– The City (New York Scene), 1920
Oil on canvas, 85.5 × 65 cm
1975.22
– Pop and the Boys, 1963
Oil on canvas, 67.8 × 47.7 cm
1976.5

**Berninghaus, Oscar Edmund
(1874-1952)**
Apache Braves, circa 1915
Watercolour, 49.5 × 34.5 cm
1982.23

Bierstadt, Albert (1830-1902)
Landscape in Yosemite Valley,
circa 1865-70
Oil on canvas, 56 × 77.6 cm
1980.13

Blümner, Oscar Julius (1867-1938)
– Red against Blue, 1933
Tempera on cardboard, 60 × 80 cm
1973.54
– Red and White, 1934
Tempera on paper, 58.5 × 81.5 cm
1974.1

Boeck, Felix de (1898-1995)
Abstract Composition, 1921
Oil on masonite panel, 60 × 68 cm
1978.82

**Bricher, Alfred Thompson
(1837-1908)**
*– Hunter in the Meadows of Old
Newburyport, Massachusetts,*
circa 1873
Oil on canvas, 56 × 112 cm
1980.83
– Low Tide at Swallow Tail Cove,
circa 1890-1900
Oil on canvas, 63.5 × 132.5 cm
1980.76

**Burchfield, Charles Ephraim
(1893-1967)**
– Haunted Evening, 1919
Watercolour on paper,
40.6 × 63.5 cm
1978.20
– Dream of a Storm at Dawn,
circa 1963-66
Watercolour on paper,
76.2 × 102 cm
1981.26

Chase, William Merritt (1849-1916)
*Child Star Elsie Leslie Lyde as Little
Lord Fauntleroy,* 1889
Oil on canvas, 176.2 × 100.3 cm
1981.27

**Chashnik, Ilja Grigorievich
(1902-1929)**
– *White Monochrome Relief,* 1922
Oil on wooden relief on plywood
panel, 100 × 147 cm
1980.2
– *Composition,* circa 1924
Watercolour and pencil on paper,
14 × 10 cm
1976.18
– *Suprematist Relief No. II,* circa 1926
Oil on wood and glass,
82.8 × 62.3 cm
1976.13
**Church, Frederic Edwin
(1826-1900)**
Iceberg and Shipwreck at Sunset,
circa 1860
Oil on paperboard and canvas,
21 × 33.7 cm
1982.10
Cole, Thomas (1801-1848)
View of the Arno, circa 1835-38
Oil on canvas, 81.5 × 130.3 cm
1980.16
Colman, Samuel (1832-1920)
View on the Hudson River,
circa 1865-69
Oil on canvas, 38.3 × 76.2 cm
1980.17

Cropsey, Jasper Francis (1823-1900)
– *Ideal Landscape: Homage to Thomas
Cole,* 1850
Oil on canvas, 20.5 × 30.7 cm
1981.47
– *View near Sherburne, Chenango
County, New York,* 1853
Oil on canvas, 61.5 × 105.2 cm
1980.18
Davis, Stuart (1894-1964)
Tao Tea Balls and Teapot, 1924
Oil on canvas, 46 × 61 cm
1983.3
De Chirico, Giorgio (1888-1978)
– *Portrait of a Young Girl
with an Apple,* 1921
Oil on canvas, 41 × 30 cm
1977.30
– *The Solitary Archaeologist,* 1966
Oil on canvas, 50 × 40 cm
1974.11
Del Marle, Félix (1889-1952)
Triptych, 1925
Oil on canvas, 162 × 67.5 cm (each)
1983.40.1-3
Demuth, Charles (1883-1935)
– *Church in Provincetown, No. 2,*
1919
Watercolour on paper, 44.5 × 34.5 cm
1973.62

– *Red and Yellow Tulips*, 1933
Watercolour on paper, 24.7 × 35 cm
1979.33
– *Zinnias*, 1933
Watercolour on paper, 33 × 25.5 cm
1979.21
Dexel, Walter (1890-1973)
Skyscraper, 1923
Oil on canvas, 65 × 46 cm
1978.76
Domela, César (1900-1992)
Composition No. 5M. Lozenge, 1926
Oil on canvas, 60 × 60 cm
1979.83
**Ender, Ksenia Vladimirovna
(1895-1955)**
– *Composition*, 1918
Oil on cardboard, 48.5 × 61.5 cm
1980.19
– *Untitled*, 1918
Oil on cardboard, 42.7 × 62 cm
1978.77
Ernst, Max (1891-1976)
– *The Sea*, 1924
Oil on canvas, 46.5 × 38.1 cm
1976.6
– *Loplop Présente la Belle Saison*, 1930
Oil on canvas, 38 × 46 cm
1977.107

– *The Red Sun*, 1957
Oil on canvas, 31 × 41.4 cm
1971.5
Estes, Richard (b. 1936)
Hotel Lucerne, 1976
Oil on canvas, 122.3 × 153 cm
1982.14
**Exter, Alexandra Alexandrovna
(1882-1949)**
Two Women in a Garden, 1927
Oil on canvas, 85 × 70 cm
1976.78
Farny, Henry Francis (1847-1916)
– *New Territory*, 1893
Gouache on paper mounted
on board, 24.8 × 40.4 cm
1980.72
– *Indian Head*, 1908
Oil on canvas, 24.1 × 16.5 cm
1980.84
– *A Moment of Suspense*, 1911
Oil on canvas, 61.3 × 41 cm
1980.4
Feininger, Lyonel (1871-1956)
– *La Belle*, 1906
Black ink on paper, 26.5 × 21 cm
1976.62

*– The Street Behind the Church.
Treptow an der Rega,* 1931
Watercolour and ink on hand-made
paper, 29.4 × 23.5 cm
1976.36
*– Magic River (Dream Across the
River),* 1937
Oil on canvas, 36 × 70 cm
1963.6
Freud, Lucian (b. 1922)
*Seated Man (Portrait of Baron H.H.
Thyssen-Bornemisza),* 1983-85
Oil on canvas, 120 × 100 cm
1985.19
**Gifford, Sanford Robinson
(1823-1880)**
– The Beach of Manchester, 1865
Oil on canvas, 28.3 × 48.5 cm
1980.21
– Stelvio Road by Lago di Como, 1868
Oil on canvas, 24.7 × 20.5 cm
1980.66
Gnoli, Domenico (1933-1970)
The Temple, 1960
Oil on canvas, 99 × 79 cm
1979.58
Hart, James McDougal (1828-1901)
Woodland Lake, 1859
Oil on canvas, 117 × 183 cm
1988.11

**Hawthorne, Charles Webster
(1872-1930)**
The Kimono Girl, circa 1898
Oil on canvas, 76.5 × 61 cm
1989.18
Heade, Martin Johnson (1819-1904)
– Two Hunters in a Landscape, 1862
Oil on canvas, 31.2 × 61 cm
1982.24
– Orchid and Two Hummingbirds,
1872
Oil on panel, 39.2 × 50.7 cm
1987.25
Henri, Robert (1865-1929)
Marjorie Reclining, 1918
Oil on canvas, 66 × 81 cm
1981.13
Hirsch, Joseph (1910-1981)
Concert, circa 1978-80
Oil and gouache on canvas,
130 × 175.2 cm
1980.7
Hodler, Ferdinand (1853-1918)
Young Man next to a River, 1901
Oil on canvas, 34 × 28 cm
1978.44
Homer, Winslow (1836-1910)
– Early Morning in the Adirondacks,
1892
Watercolour on paper, 40 × 56 cm
1977.109

– Gallow's Island, Bermuda,
circa 1899-1901
Watercolour on paper, 34.5 × 52 cm
1977.7
Hopper, Edward (1882-1967)
– My Roof, 1928
Watercolour on paper, 35 × 50 cm
1977.8
– Rocky Cove, 1929
Watercolour on paper,
34.2 × 49.5 cm
1977.81
Itten, Johannes (1888-1967)
Kindly Light, 1963
Oil on canvas, 100 × 72 cm
1964.10
Jawlensky, Alexej von (1864-1941)
Child with a Doll, 1910
Oil on board, 61 × 50.5 cm
1983.14
Johnson, David (1827-1908)
View of the Androscoggin River, Maine,
1869-70
Oil on canvas, 71 × 112 cm
1981.44
Johnson, Eastman (1824-1906)
Girl at the Window, circa 1870
Oil on cardboard, 67.3 × 55.9 cm
1980.23

**Kakabadze, David Nestorovich
(1889-1952)**
Untitled, 1920
Oil on cardboard, 52 × 61.5 cm
1983.34
Kensett, John Frederick (1816-1872)
– Landscape, 1851
Oil on canvas, 75.5 × 63.5 cm
1985.23
– The Trout Fisherman, 1852
Oil on canvas, 48.5 × 40.6 cm
1980.52
Kliun, Ivan Vasilievich (1870-1942)
Untitled, 1921
Tempera on cardboard, 22 × 26.4 cm
1978.91
Krasner, Lee (1908-1984)
Red, White, Blue, Yellow, Black, 1939
Collage and oil on paper, 63 × 48 cm
1978.9
Kuhn, Walt (1877-1949)
Chorus Captain, 1935
Oil on canvas, 102 × 76.2 cm
1979.35
Larionov, Mikhail (1881-1964)
The Brawl, 1911
Oil on canvas, 71.3 × 94 cm
1987.17

Lawson, Ernest (1873-1939)
Stream by the Farm, circa 1902
Oil on canvas, 50.8 × 61 cm
1979.72
**Lebedev, Vladimir Vasilievich
(1891-1967)**
Cubism: A Portrait, circa 1920
Oil on canvas, 85 × 68 cm
1983.35.b
Léger, Fernand (1881-1955)
Man and Woman, 1921
Watercolour, 36.5 × 26.5 cm
1976.94
**Leigh, William Robinson
(1866-1955)**
Indian Herder, 1912
Tempera on board, 67.3 × 49.5 cm
1981.45
Lindner, Richard (1901-1978)
Out of Towners, 1968
Pencil and red ink on paper,
60 × 50 cm
1973.27
Macke, August (1887-1914)
Flowers, circa 1913
Watercolour, Indian and coloured
inks on paper, 28.5 × 23.5 cm
1969.9

**Malevich, Kazimir Severinovich
(1878-1935)**
Untitled, circa 1919
Gouache on paper, 31.7 × 23.8 cm
1980.53
Mansouroff, Paul (1896-1984)
– *Painterly Formula*, circa 1918
Oil on panel, 133 × 26.9 cm
1977.114
– *Untitled*, circa 1923-24
Oil on panel, 127 × 40.8 cm
1983.5
Marc, Franz (1880-1916)
Cup with a Fox and a Deer, 1915
Mixed media, 15.7 × 12.2 cm
1975.32
Marin, John (1870-1953)
– *New York Series*, 1927
Watercolour and tempera on paper,
67 × 54 cm
1981.9
– *Eastport, Maine*, 1933
Watercolour on paper, 43 × 33.6 cm
1979.70
Marini, Marino (1901-1980)
Rider on a Red Horse, 1952
Indian ink and gouache on paper,
60 × 39 cm
1963.4

Marsh, Reginald (1898-1954)
Food Store (The Death of Dillinger),
1938
Tempera on board, 71.1 × 50.8 cm
1978.24
Masson, André (1896-1987)
The Statue, 1925
Oil on canvas, 55 × 35 cm
1975.17
Moran, Thomas (1837-1926)
Windsor Castle, 1883
Oil on canvas, 93.5 × 152.8 cm
1981.22
**Mount, William Sidney
(1807-1869)**
The Stone Bridge, 1843
Oil on board, 20.3 × 32.5 cm
1982.48
Müller, Otto (1874-1930)
Nude by a Woodland Pool,
circa 1920-22
Watercolour and crayon on paper,
50 × 34 cm
1974.56
**Murillo, Bartolomé Esteban
(1618-1682)**
St. Francis in Ecstasy, circa 1650-55
Oil on canvas, 168.7 × 113 cm
1990.7

Nolde, Emil (1867-1956)
– *Flower Garden*, 1917
Oil on plywood panel,
82.5 × 64.5 cm
1964.8
– *Head of a Woman*, circa 1925-30
Watercolour on paper, 47 × 34.5 cm
1970.34
– *Summer Flowers (Red and White
Poppies against a Blue Sky)*, circa 1930
Watercolour on paper,
45.5 × 33.5 cm
1965.5
– *Iris, Tiger-Lilies, Poppies*,
circa 1930-35
Watercolour on paper, 47 × 34 cm
1970.31
– *Young Couple*, circa 1931-35
Watercolour on paper laid on card,
53.5 × 37 cm
1961.3
– *Landscape with Farms*, 1946-47
Watercolour on paper,
22.5 × 26.3 cm
1974.24
Ossorio, Alfonso Angel (b. 1916)
The Cross in the Garden, 1950
Mixed media and collage on paper,
75.8 × 55.3 cm
1981.3

Parrish, David (b. 1939)
Three Yamahas, 1976
Oil on canvas, 165 × 165 cm
1976.84
Pène du Bois, Guy (1884-1958)
– *Le Viol*, circa 1927
Oil on canvas, 101.6 × 76.2 cm
1979.85
– *42nd Street* , 1945
Oil on canvas, 81.5 × 66 cm
1981.29
Picabia, Francis (1879-1953)
Le Broyeur, 1921-22
Pencil, watercolour and gouache,
60 × 73 cm
1976.96
Pollock, Jackson (1912-1956)
– *Untitled*, circa 1945
Pastel, brush and enamel, and
sgraffito on paper, 65 × 52 cm
1978.18
– *Untitled*, 1946
Gouache on paper, 56.3 × 77.5 cm
1976.37
– *Number 11*, 1950
Oil and aluminium paint
on masonite, 56.5 × 56.5 cm
1975.28

Pousette-Dart, Richard (1916-1992)
Composition, circa 1942
Oil on canvas, 112 × 94 cm
1975.42
**Pynas, Jan Symonsz (1583/4-1631),
attributed to**
Joseph Meeting Jacob in Egypt, 1618
Oil on canvas, 165.7 × 231.1 cm
1994.17
Ray, Man (1890-1976)
The Keyhole, 1928
Oil on canvas, 45.7 × 38.1 cm
1979.16
Remington, Frederic (1861-1909)
*The Parley (Questionable
Companionship)*, circa 1903
Oil on canvas, 68.5 × 102 cm
1981.7
Riopelle, Jean-Paul (b. 1923)
Composition, n.d.
Oil on canvas, 95.5 × 127.5 cm
1976.51
Roberts, William (1895-1980)
– *War Celebration*, 1919
Pencil, pen, ink and watercolour,
43.1 × 35.6 cm
1981.23
– *Dock Gates*, 1920
Oil on canvas, 92 × 122 cm
1982.44

Robinson, Theodore (1852-1896)
– *On the Cliff (Girl Sewing)*, 1887
Oil on panel, 23.9 × 32.3 cm
1979.17
– *In the Garden*, circa 1891
Oil on canvas, 46 × 55.5 cm
1981.59
Röhl, Karl Peter (1890-1975)
Black-Blue (Large Square), 1922
Ink and gouache on paper,
52 × 38.5 cm
1986.19
**Rozanova, Olga Vladimirovna
(1886-1918)**
Urban Landscape, 1912
Oil on cardboard, 61 × 51 cm
1980.25
Schiele, Egon (1890-1918)
Boy in a Sailor Suit (Paul Erdmann),
1915
Graphite, wax crayon and oil paint
on drawing paper, 47.5 × 31.5 cm
1974.18
Schmidt-Rottluff, Karl (1884-1976)
The Village of Dangast, 1909
Watercolour on paper,
52.5 × 65.5 cm
1970.28

Segal, Arthur (1875-1944)
Bridge, 1921
Oil on canvas and wooden frame,
85.5 × 105.5 cm
1978.80
Severini, Gino (1883-1966)
– *Still Life with a Bottle of Marsala*,
1917
Oil on cardboard, 46 × 33 cm
1976.10
– *Pas de Deux No. 1*, 1950
Oil on canvas, 116 × 89 cm
1976.27
Shahn, Ben (1898-1969)
Riot on Carol Street, 1944
Tempera on board, 71 × 51 cm
1977.10
Sheeler, Charles (1883-1965)
– *Ore into Iron*, 1953
Tempera on plexiglass, 23 × 17.2 cm
1973.8
– *Composition around Yellow No. 2*,
1958
Tempera on paper, 14 × 18 cm
1973.7
**Stepanova, Varvara Fedorovna
(1894-1958)**
Two People at a Table, 1921
Tempera and pencil on paper,
28.7 × 28.5 cm
1983.28

Tàpies, Antonio (b. 1923)
Untitled, circa 1965
Ink and sepia on paper, 65 × 90 cm
1972.7
**Thompson, Alfred Wordsworth
(1840-1896)**
The Garden at Monte Carlo, 1876-77
Oil on canvas, 48.3 × 82 cm
1979.51
**Toulouse-Lautrec, Henri de
(1864-1901)**
*– At the Moulin Rouge: La Goulue
and Her Sister,* 1892
Colour lithograph, 45.5 × 34.7 cm
1973.40
– Englishman at the Moulin Rouge,
1892
Colour lithograph, 48 × 37.8 cm
1973.33
*– Englishman at the Moulin Rouge
No. 92,* 1892
Colour lithograph, 52.5 × 37.2 cm
1973.33
– Mademoiselle Marcelle Lender, 1895
Colour lithograph, 36 × 24.7 cm
1973.39
*– The Sitting Female Clown:
Mademoiselle Cha-U-Kao,* 1896
Colour lithograph, 52 × 40.5 cm
1973.34

– La Grande Loge, 1897
Colour lithograph, 51 × 41 cm
1973.41
– The Dance at the Moulin Rouge,
1897
Colour lithograph, 45.5 × 36 cm
1973.36
– Elsa, la Viennoise, 1897
Colour lithograph, 58 × 39.5 cm
1973.37
*– The Female Clown at the Moulin
Rouge,* 1897
Colour lithograph, 41.2 × 32.3 cm
1973.35
– The Jockey, 1899
Colour lithograph, 51.5 × 36.2 cm
1973.38
**Udaltsova, Nadezhda Andreevna
(1886-1961)**
– Composition, 1916
Gouache, watercolour and pencil
on brown wrapping paper,
46.8 × 37.8 cm
1980.26
– Untitled, 1917
Gouache, watercolour and pencil
on thick paper, 36 × 25 cm
1977.105

Vassilieff, Marie (1884-1957)
Woman with a Fan, 1910
Oil on canvas, 60 × 72.5 cm
1978.79
Weber, Max (1881-1961)
New York, 1913
Oil on canvas, 101.6 × 81.3 cm
1977.112
Weir, Julian Alden (1852-1919)
Silver Chalice with Roses, 1882
Oil on canvas, 31.5 × 23 cm
1980.54
**Whittredge, Thomas Worthington
(1820-1910)**
— Valley of the Ocale, 1865
Oil on paper mounted on cardboard,
20.5 × 58.5 cm
1983.33
— Autumn on the Hudson River,
circa 1875
Oil on canvas, 50.5 × 68 cm
1980.11
— A Catskill Brook, circa 1875
Oil on canvas, 77 × 113.7 cm
1987.27
Wiles, Irving Ramsey (1861-1948)
Woman Reading on a Bench,
circa 1895
Oil on panel, 35 × 43.7 cm
1979.23

Wit, Jacob de (1695-1754)
— St. Augustine
Oil on canvas, 85 × 222 × 2 cm
1996.3.1
— St. Luke
Oil on canvas, 84 × 156 × 2 cm
1996.3.2
— St. James
Oil on canvas, 83 × 184 × 2 cm
1996.3.3
— St. Giuda Taddeo
Oil on canvas, 85 × 186 × 2 cm
1996.3.4
— St. John the Evangelist
Oil on canvas, 85 × 105.5 × 2 cm
1996.3.5
— St. Mark
Oil on canvas, 85 × 158 × 2 cm
1996.3.6
— St. Matthew
Oil on canvas, 85 × 105.5 × 2 cm
1996.3.7
— St. Ambrose
Oil on canvas, 84 × 156 × 2 cm
1996.3.8
— St. Jerome
Oil on canvas, 84 × 120 × 2 cm
1996.3.9
— St. Gregory
Oil on canvas, 85 × 158 × 2 cm
1996.3.10

Wyeth, Andrew (b. 1917)
Malamute, 1976
Watercolour on paper, 79 × 137 cm
1977.84

Archipenko, Alexander (1887-1964)
Queen of Sheba, 1961
Bronze with gold patina, H 165 cm
DEC1687
Barlach, Ernst (1870-1938)
The Terrorized, 1912
Bronze, 47 × 44.5 × 29 cm
DEC1689
Benedetto da Maiano (1442-1497)
– *St. John the Evangelist*, 1450-1500
Terracotta, traces of polychromy,
H 94.2 cm
DEC1953
– *Madonna and Child with Angels*
(copy from a model by), late 16th
century
Terracotta glazed in polychrome,
relief diameter 53.5 cm
Frame: workshop of Giovanni della
Robbia (1469-1529/30), Florence,
circa 1525, diameter 82 cm
DEC1590
Bracci, Pietro (1700-1773)
Pope Benedict XIII, circa 1762-73
Marble, H (with socle): 93.1 cm;
(without socle): 76.4 cm
DEC1615

Donatello (1386-1466)
(from a model by)
Virgin and Child, circa 1450
Painted stucco, 85 × 57 cm
DEC1580
Hepworth, Barbara (1903-1975)
Orpheus (Maquette I), 1956
Brass with strings on wooden base,
H 42 cm
DEC1702
Huf, Fritz (1888-1970)
– *Cubistic Sculpture*, 1930
Plaster of Paris, H 16 cm
DEC1703
– *Oblique/Abstract Sculpture*, 1956
Bronze, H 21.5 cm, pedestal 4 cm
DEC1704
**Jorhan, Christian, the Elder
(1727-1804), workshop of**
Female Saint, circa 1775-80
Limewood, painted and gilt,
H 180 cm
DEC1669
**Klahr, Michael (1693-1743),
workshop of**
Pair of Angels, circa 1725-30
Limewood, painted white, H 166 cm
(left angel), H 184 cm (right angel)
DEC1670.1-2

Lehmbruck, Wilhelm (1881-1919)
Venus, 20th century
Bronze with wood gilt base, H 54 cm
DEC1706
Pevsner, Anton (1884-1962)
*Construction Spatiale aux Troisième
et Quatrième Dimensions*, 1961
Bronze with gold patina, H 100 cm
DEC1715
**Romano, Gian Cristoforo
(1465-1512)**
Isabella d'Este, Marchioness of Mantua,
circa 1498
Terracotta, formerly polychromed,
54.3 cm × 54.6 cm
DEC1578
**Rossellino, Antonio (1427-1479),
in the manner of**
Virgin and Child, early 20th century
Marble, 80 × 55.5 cm
DEC1598
**Tribolo, Niccolò (1500-1550),
in the manner of**
Boy Sitting on a Pitcher, mid 16th
century
Marble, H 57.6 cm
DEC1575

Unknown
– *Madonna and Child*, 1300-50
Wood with original polychromy,
101 × 25 cm
DEC1625
– *The Education of the Virgin*,
mid 14th century
Oak, with traces of polychromy,
H 95 cm
DEC1626
– *St. Anne, the Virgin and the Christ
Child*, circa 1480-1500
Oak, remains of polychromy,
100 × 60 cm
DEC1650
– *St. Florian*, circa 1515-20
Limewood, remains of polychromy,
92.5 × 36 × 28 cm
DEC1659
– *St. Michael*, circa 1500-10
Limewood, leached, traces of
polychromy, 131.5 × 60 × 23 cm
DEC1662
– *Tapestry with Donor in Prayer*
(fragment)
Germany (Franconia), circa 1430
Wool and silk, 89 × 55 cm
DEC0575

Zadkine, Ossip (1890-1967)
Deux Amies, 1957
Bronze with gold patina, H 64 cm
DEC1719